*"One of the brightest minds in finance."* **CNBC (6/11/10)**

*"Warren Mosler is one of the most original and clear-eyed participants in today's debates over economic policy."*
**JAMES GALBRAITH, FORMER EXECUTIVE DIRECTOR, JOINT ECONOMIC COMMITTEE AND PROFESSOR, THE UNIVERSITY OF TEXAS - AUSTIN**

*"I can say without hesitation that Warren Mosler has had the most profound impact on our understanding of modern money and government budgets of anyone I know or know of, including Nobel Prize winners, Central Bank Directors, Ministers of Finance and full professors at Ivy League Universities. It is no exaggeration to say that his ideas concerning economic theory and policy are responsible for the most exciting new paradigm in economics in the last 30 years - perhaps longer - and he has inspired more economists to turn their attention to the real world of economic policy than any other single individual."*
**DR. MATTHEW FORSTATER, PROFESSOR OF ECONOMICS, UNIVERSITY OF MISSOURI - KANSAS CITY**

*"Warren is one of the rare individuals who understand money and finance and how the Treasury and the Fed really work. He receives information from industry experts from all over the world."*
**WILLIAM K. BLACK, ASSOCIATE PROFESSOR OF ECONOMICS & LAW, UNIVERSITY OF MISSOURI - KANSAS CITY**

*"He [Warren Mosler] represents a rare combination: someone who combines an exceptional knowledge of finance with the wisdom and compassion required to get us an array of policies that will bring us back to sustainable full employment."*
**MARSHALL AUERBACK, GLOBAL PORTFOLIO STRATEGIST, RAB CAPITAL AND FELLOW, ECONOMISTS FOR PEACE & SECURITY**

*"In this book, Warren Mosler borrows John Kenneth Galbraith's notion of 'innocent fraud' and identifies seven of the most destructive yet widely held myths about the economy. Like Galbraith, Mosler chooses to accept the possibility that the fraud is unintentional, resulting from ignorance, misunderstanding or, most likely, from application of the wrong economic paradigm to*

*our real world economy. To put it as simply as possible, many of the most dangerous beliefs about the way the economy functions would have some relevance if the U.S. were on a strict gold standard. Yet, obviously, the U.S. dollar has had no link whatsoever to gold since the break-up of the Bretton Woods system.*

*So what are the deadly (yet perhaps innocent) frauds? First, government finance is supposed to be similar to household finance: government needs to tax and borrow first before it can spend. Second, today's deficits burden our grandchildren with government debt. Third, worse, deficits absorb today's saving. Fourth, Social Security has promised pensions and healthcare that it will never be able to afford. Fifth, the U.S. trade deficit reduces domestic employment and dangerously indebts Americans to the whims of foreigners - who might decide to cut off the supply of loans that we need. Sixth, and related to fraud number three, we need savings to finance investment (so government budgets lead to less investment). And, finally, higher budget deficits imply taxes will have to be higher in the future - adding to the burden on future taxpayers.*

*Mosler shows that whether or not these beliefs are innocent, they are most certainly wrong. Again, there might be some sort of economy in which they could be more-or-less correct. For example, in a nonmonetary economy, a farmer needs to save seed corn to 'invest' it in next year's rop. On a gold standard, a government really does need to tax and borrow to ensure it can maintain a fixed exchange rate. And so on. But in the case of nonconvertible currency (in the sense that government does not promise to convert at a fixed exchange rate to precious metal or foreign currency), none of these myths holds. Each is a fraud.*

*The best reason to read this book is to ensure that you can recognize a fraud when you hear one. And in his clear and precise style, Mosler will introduce you to the correct paradigm to develop an understanding of the world in which we actually live."*

**L. RANDALL WRAY, PROFESSOR OF ECONOMICS, UNIVERSITY OF MISSOURI - KANSAS CITY, RESEARCH DIRECTOR, CENTER FOR FULL EMPLOYMENT & PRICE STABILITY, SENIOR SCHOLAR, LEVY ECONOMICS INSTITUTE, AUTHOR OF** *UNDERSTANDING MODERN MONEY, THE KEY TO FULL EMPLOYMENT AND PRICE STABILITY* **AND EDITOR,** *CREDIT AND STATE THEORIES OF MONEY: THE CONTRIBUTIONS OF A. MITCHELL INNES*

# WRITINGS of WARREN MOSLER
(found on *www.moslereconomics.com_*
and *www.mosler.org*)

The Seven Deadly Innocent Frauds of Economic Policy

Galbraith/Wray/Mosler submission for February 25

Mosler Palestinian Development Plan

Soft Currency Economics

Full Employment AND Price Stability

A General Analytical Framework for the Analysis of Currencies and
Other Commodities

The Natural Rate of Interest is Zero

2004 Proposal for Senator Lieberman

An Interview with the Chairman

The Innocent Fraud of the Trade Deficit: Who's Funding Whom?

The Financial Crisis - Views and Remedies

Quantitative Easing for Dummies

Tax-Driven Money

# SEVEN DEADLY INNOCENT FRAUDS OF ECONOMIC POLICY

WARREN MOSLER

VALANCE CO., INC.

Library of Congress Cataloging-in-Publication Data in progress for

ISBN: 978-0-692-00959-8

The text of this book is set in 12 pt. Times. Printed & bound in the U.S.A.

16 15 14 13 12 11 10      10 9 8 7 6 5 4 3 2 1

FIRST IMPRESSION

VALANCE CO., INC.

# CONTENTS

# Foreword

Warren Mosler is a rare bird: a self-taught economist who is not a crank; a successful investor who is not a blowhard; a businessperson with a talent for teaching; a financier with a true commitment to the public good.

We have co-authored testimony and the occasional article, and I attest firmly that his contributions to those efforts exceeded mine.

Many economists value complexity for its own sake. A glance at any modern economics journal confirms this. A truly incomprehensible argument can bring a lot of prestige! The problem, though, is that when an argument appears incomprehensible, that often means the person making it doesn't understand it either. (I was just at a meeting of European central bankers and international monetary economists in Helsinki, Finland. After one paper, I asked a very distinguished economist from Sweden how many people he thought had followed the math. He said, "Zero.") Warren's gift is transparent lucidity. He thinks things through as simply as he can. (And he puts a lot of work into this - true simplicity is hard.) He favors the familiar metaphor, and the homely example. You can explain his reasoning to most children (at least to mine), to any college student and to any player in the financial markets. Only economists, with their powerful loyalty to fixed ideas, have trouble with it. Politicians, of course, often do understand, but rarely feel free to speak their own minds.

Now comes Warren Mosler with a small book, setting out his reasoning on seven key issues. These relate to government deficits and debt, to the relation between public deficits and

1

private savings, to that between savings and investment, to Social Security and to the trade deficit. Warren calls them "Seven Deadly Innocent Frauds" - taking up a phrase coined by my father as the title of his last book. Galbraith-the-elder would have been pleased.

The common thread tying these themes together is simplicity itself. It's that modern money is a spreadsheet! It works by computer! When government spends or lends, it does so by adding numbers to private bank accounts. When it taxes, it marks those same accounts down. When it borrows, it shifts funds from a demand deposit (called a reserve account) to savings (called a securities account). And that for practical purposes is all there is. The money government spends doesn't come from anywhere, and it doesn't cost anything to produce. The government therefore cannot run out.

Money is created by government spending (or by bank loans, which create deposits). Taxes serve to make us want that money - we need it in order to pay the taxes. And they help regulate total spending, so that we don't have more total spending than we have goods available at current prices - something that would force up prices and cause inflation. But taxes aren't needed in advance of spending - and could hardly be, since before the government spends there is no money to tax.

A government borrowing in its own currency need never default on its debts; paying them is simply a matter of adding the interest to the bank accounts of the bond holders. A government can only decide to default – an act of financial suicide – or (in the case of a government borrowing in a currency it doesn't control) be forced to default by its bankers. But a U.S. bank will always cash a check issued by the US Government, whatever happens.

2

Nor is the public debt a burden on the future. How could it be? Everything produced in the future will be consumed in the future. How much will be produced depends on how productive the economy is at that time. This has nothing to do with the public debt today; a higher public debt today does not reduce future production - and if it motivates wise use of resources today, it may increase the productivity of the economy in the future.

Public deficits increase financial private savings - as a matter of accounting, dollar for dollar. Imports are a benefit, exports a cost. We do not borrow from China to finance our consumption: the borrowing that finances an import from China is done by a U.S. consumer at a U.S. bank. Social Security privatization would just reshuffle the ownership of stocks and bonds in the economy – transferring risky assets to seniors and safer ones to the wealthy – without having any other economic effects. The Federal Reserve sets interest rates where it wants.

All these are among the simple principles set out in this small book.

Also included here are an engaging account of the education of a financier and an action program for saving the American economy from the crisis of high unemployment. Warren would do this by suspending the payroll tax – giving every working American a raise of over 8 percent, after tax; by a per capita grant to state and local governments, to cure their fiscal crises; and by a public employment program offering a job at a modest wage to anyone who wanted one. This would eliminate the dangerous forms of unemployment and allow us to put our young people, especially, to useful work.

3

Warren's heroes, among economists and apart from my father, are Wynne Godley and Abba Lerner. Godley – a wonderful man who just passed away – prefigured much of this work with his stock-flow consistent macroeconomic models, which have proved to be among the best forecasting tools in the business. Lerner championed "functional finance," meaning that public policy should be judged by its results in the real world - employment, productivity and price stability - and not by whatever may be happening to budget and debt numbers. Warren also likes to invoke Lerner's Law - the principle that, in economics, one should never compromise principles, no matter how much trouble other people have in understanding them. I wish I were as a good at observing that principle as he is.

All in all, this book is an engaging and highly instructive read - highly recommended.

James K. Galbraith
The University of Texas at Austin
June 12, 2010

# Prologue

The term *"innocent fraud"* was introduced by Professor John Kenneth Galbraith in his last book, **The Economics of Innocent Fraud**, which he wrote at the age of ninety-four in 2004, just two years before he died. Professor Galbraith coined the term to describe a variety of incorrect assumptions embraced by mainstream economists, the media and, most of all, politicians.

The presumption of innocence, yet another example of Galbraith's elegant and biting wit, implies that those perpetuating the fraud are not only wrong but also not clever enough to understand what they are actually doing. And any claim of prior understanding becomes an admission of deliberate fraud - an unthinkable self-incrimination.

Galbraith's economic views gained a wide audience during the 1950s and 1960s with his best-selling books, **The Affluent Society** and **The New Industrial State**. He was well connected to both the Kennedy and Johnson administrations, serving as the United States Ambassador to India from 1961 until 1963, when he returned to his post as Harvard's most renowned Professor of Economics.

Galbraith was largely a Keynesian who believed that only fiscal policy can restore "spending power." Fiscal policy is what economists call tax cuts and spending increases, and spending in general is what they call "aggregate demand."

Galbraith's academic antagonist, Milton Friedman, led another school of thought known as "monetarist." The monetarists believe that the federal government should always keep the budget in balance and use "monetary policy" to regulate the economy. Initially, that meant keeping the money supply growing slowly and steadily to control inflation and letting the economy do what it may. However, they never could come up with a measure of money supply that did the trick. Nor could the Federal Reserve ever find a way to actually control the measures of money with which they experimented.

Paul Volcker was the last Fed Chairman to attempt to directly control the money supply. After a prolonged period of actions that merely demonstrated what most central bankers had known for a very long time - that there was no such thing as controlling the money supply - Volcker abandoned the effort.

Monetary policy was quickly redefined as a policy of using interest rates as the instrument of monetary policy rather than any measure of the quantity of money. And "inflation expectations" moved to the top of the list as the cause of inflation, as the money supply no longer played an active role. Interestingly, "money" doesn't appear anywhere in the latest monetarist mathematical models that advocate the use of interest rates to regulate the economy.

Whenever there are severe economic slumps, politicians need results - in the form of more jobs - to stay in office. First, they watch as the Federal Reserve cuts interest rates, waiting patiently for the low rates to somehow "kick in." Unfortunately, interest rates never seem to "kick in." Then, as rising unemployment threatens the re-election of members of Congress and the President, the politicians turn to Keynesian policies of tax cuts and spending increases. These policies are implemented over the intense objections and dire predictions of the majority of central bankers and mainstream economists.

It was Richard Nixon who famously declared during the double-dip economic slump of 1973, "We are all Keynesians now."

Despite Nixon's statement, Galbraith's Keynesian views lost out to the monetarists when the "great inflation" of the 1970s sent shock waves through the American psyche. Public policy turned to the Federal Reserve and its manipulation of interest rates as the most effective way to deal with what was coined "stagflation," the combination of a stagnant economy and high inflation.

I entered banking in 1973 with a job collecting delinquent loans at the Savings Bank of Manchester in my home town of Manchester, Connecticut. I was the bank's portfolio manager by 1975, which led to Wall St. in 1976, where I worked on the trading floor until 1978. Then I was hired by William Blair and Company in Chicago to add fixed income arbitrage to their corporate bond department. It was from there that I started my own fund in 1982. I saw the great inflation as a cost-push phenomena driven by OPEC's pricing power. It had every appearance of a cartel setting ever-higher prices which caused the great inflation, and a simple supply response that broke it. As OPEC raised the nominal price of crude oil from $2 per barrel in the early 1970s to a peak of about $40 per barrel approximately 10 years later, I could see two possible outcomes. The first was for it to somehow be kept to a relative value story, where U.S. inflation remained fairly low and paying more for oil and gasoline simply meant less demand and weaker prices for most everything else, with wages and salaries staying relatively constant. This would have meant a drastic reduction in real terms of trade and standard of living for the oil exporters.

The second outcome, which is what happened, was for a general inflation to ensue. So while OPEC did get higher prices for its oil, they also had to pay higher prices for what they wanted to buy, leaving real terms of trade not all that different after the price of oil finally settled between $10 and $5 per barrel, where it remained for over a decade. And from where I sat, I didn't see any deflationary consequences from the "tight" monetary policy. Instead, it was the deregulation of natural gas in 1978 that allowed natural gas prices to rise, and therefore, natural gas wells to be uncapped. U.S. electric utility companies then switched fuels from high-priced oil to what was still lower-priced natural gas. OPEC reacted to this supply response by rapidly cutting production in an attempt to keep prices from falling below $30 per oil barrel. Production was cut by over 15 million barrels a day, but it wasn't enough, and they drowned in the sea of excess world oil production as electric utilities continued to move to other fuels.

This book is divided into three sections Part one immediately reveals the seven "innocent frauds" that I submit are the most imbedded obstacles to national prosperity. They are presented in a manner that does not require any prior knowledge or understanding of the monetary system, economics or accounting. The first three concern the federal government's budget deficit, the fourth addresses Social Security, the fifth international trade. the sixth savings and investment and the seventh returns to the federal budget deficit. This last chapter is the core message; its purpose is to promote a universal understanding of these critical issues facing our nation.

Part two is the evolution of my awareness of these seven deadly innocent frauds during my more-than-three decades of experience in the world of finance.

In Part three, I apply the knowledge of the seven deadly innocent frauds to the leading issues of the day.

In Part four, I set forth a specific action plan for our country to realize our economic potential and restore the American dream.

April 15, 2010
Warren Mosler
67 Chimney Corner Circle
Guilford, CT  06437-3134

# OVERVIEW

## Seven Deadly Innocent Frauds of Economic Policy

1. The government must raise funds through taxation or borrowing in order to spend. In other words, government spending is limited by its ability to tax or borrow.

2. With government deficits, we are leaving our debt burden to our children.

3. Government budget deficits take away savings.

4. Social Security is broken.

5. The trade deficit is an unsustainable imbalance that takes away jobs and output.

6. We need savings to provide the funds for investment.

7. It's a bad thing that higher deficits today mean higher taxes tomorrow.

# Introduction

This book's purpose is to promote the restoration of American prosperity. It is my contention that the seven deadly innocent frauds of economic policy are all that is standing between today's economic mess and the full restoration of American prosperity.

As of the publication of this book, I am campaigning for the office of U.S. Senator from my home state of Connecticut, solely as a matter of conscience. I am running to promote my national agenda to restore American prosperity with the following three proposals.

The first is what's called a "full payroll tax holiday" whereby the U.S. Treasury stops taking some $20 billion EACH WEEK from people working for a living and instead, makes all FICA payments for both employees and employers. The average American couple earning a combined $100,000 per year will see their take-home pay go up by over $650 PER MONTH which will help them meet their mortgage payments and stay in their homes, which would also end the financial crisis. Additionally, the extra take-home pay would help everyone pay their bills and go shopping, as Americans return to what used to be our normal way of life.

My second proposal is for the federal government to distribute $500 per capita of revenue sharing to the state governments, with no strings attached, to tide them over and help them sustain their essential services. The spending power and millions of jobs funded by people's spending from the extra take-home pay from the payroll-tax holiday restores economic activity, and the States' revenues would return to where they were before the crisis.

My third proposal calls for a restoration of American prosperity through a federally-funded $8/hr. job for anyone willing and able to work. The primary purpose of this program is to provide a transition from unemployment to private-sector employment. A payroll-tax holiday and the state revenue-sharing would bring an immediate flurry of economic activity, with private-sector employers quickly seeking to hire millions of additional workers to meet growing demand for their products. Unfortunately, past recessions have shown that businesses are reluctant to hire those who have been unemployed, with the long-term unemployed being the least attractive. Transitional employment also would draw these people into the labor force, giving them a chance to demonstrate what they can do, and show that they are responsible and can get to work on time. This includes giving the opportunity of work to many of those who have a harder time finding private-sector employment, including high-risk teenagers, people getting out of prison, the disabled and older as well as middle-aged people who have lost their jobs and exhausted their unemployment benefits. While this program would involve the lowest expenditure of my three proposals, it is equally important as it helps smooth and optimize the transition to private-sector employment as the economy grows.

So, how am I uniquely qualified to be promoting these proposals? My confidence comes from 40 years' experience in the financial and economic realm. I would venture that I'm perhaps the only person who can answer the question: "How are you going to pay for it?" My book takes on this issue and encourages the return of economics study to the operational realities of our monetary system.

## **Part I:** The Seven Deadly Innocent Frauds

### *Deadly Innocent Fraud #1:*

The federal government must raise funds through taxation or borrowing in order to spend. In other words, government spending is limited by its ability to tax or borrow.

### *Fact:*

Federal government spending is in no case operationally constrained by revenues, meaning that **there is no "solvency risk."** In other words, the federal government can always make any and all payments in its own currency, no matter how large the deficit is, or how few taxes it collects.

Ask any congressman (as I have many times) or private citizen how it all works, and he or she will tell you emphatically that: "...the government has to either tax or borrow to get the funds to spend, just like any household has to somehow get the money it needs to spend." And from this comes the inevitable question about healthcare, defense, social security, and any and all government spending:

### **How are you going to pay for it???!!!**

This is the killer question, the one no one gets right, and getting the answer to this question right is the core of the public purpose behind writing this book.

In the next few moments of reading, it will all be revealed to you with no theory and no philosophy- just a few hard cold facts. I answer this question by first looking at exactly how government taxes, followed by how government spends.

## How does the Federal Government Tax?

Let's start by looking at what happens if you pay your taxes by writing a check. When the U.S. government gets your check, and it's deposited and "clears," all the government does is change the number in your checking account "downward" as they subtract the amount of your check from your bank balance. Does the government actually get anything real to give to someone else? No, it's not like there's a gold coin to spend. You can actually see this happen with online banking - watch the balance in your bank account on your computer screen. Suppose the balance in your account is $5,000 and you write a check to the government for $2,000. When that checks clears (gets processed), what happens? The 5 turns into a 3 and your new balance is now down to $3,000. All before your very eyes! The government didn't actually "get" anything to give to someone else. No gold coin dropped into a bucket at the Fed. They just changed numbers in bank accounts - nothing "went" anywhere.

And what happens if you were to go to your local IRS office to pay your taxes with actual cash? First, you would hand over your pile of currency to the person on duty as payment. Next, he'd count it, give you a receipt and, hopefully, a thank you for helping to pay for social security, interest on the national debt, and the Iraq war. Then, after you, the tax payer, left the room, he'd take that hard-earned cash you just forked over and **throw it in a shredder.**

Yes, it gets thrown it away. Destroyed! Why? There's no further use for it. Just like a ticket to the Super Bowl. After you enter the stadium and hand the attendant a ticket that was worth maybe $1000, he tears it up and discards it. In fact, you can actually buy shredded money in Washington, D.C.

So if the government throws away your cash after collecting it, how does that cash pay for anything, like Social Security and the rest of the government's spending? It doesn't.

Can you now see why it makes no sense at all to think that the government has to get money by taxing in order to spend? In no case does it actually "get" anything that it subsequently "uses." So if the government doesn't actually get anything when it taxes, how and what does it spend?

### How the Federal Government Spends

Imagine you are expecting your $2,000 Social Security payment to hit your bank account, which already has $3,000 in it. If you are watching your account on the computer screen, you can see how government spends without having anything to spend. Presto! Suddenly your account statement that read $3,000 now reads $5,000. What did the government do to give you that money? It simply changed the number in your bank account from 3,000 to 5,000. It didn't take a gold coin and hammer it into a computer. All it did was change a number in your bank account by making data entries on its own spreadsheet, which is linked to other spreadsheets in the banking system. Government spending is all done by data entry on its own spreadsheet called "The U.S. dollar monetary system."

Here is a quote from the good Federal Reserve Bank Chairman, Ben Bernanke, on *60 Minutes* for support:

*SCOTT PELLEY: Is that tax money that the Fed is spending?*

*CHAIRMAN BERNANKE: It's not tax money. The banks have accounts with the Fed, much the same way that you have an account in a commercial bank. So, to lend to a bank, we simply use the computer to mark up the size of the account that they have with the Fed.*

The Chairman of the Federal Reserve Bank is telling us in plain English that they give out money (spend and lend) simply by changing numbers in bank accounts. There is no such thing as having to "get" taxes (or borrow) to make a spreadsheet entry that we call "government spending." Computer data doesn't come from anywhere. Everyone knows that!

Where else do we see this happen? Your team kicks a field goal and on the scoreboard, the score changes from, say, 7 points to 10 points. Does anyone wonder where the stadium got those three points? Of course not! Or you knock down 5 pins at the bowling alley and your score goes from 10 to 15. Do you worry about where the bowling alley got those points? Do you think all bowling alleys and football stadiums should have a 'reserve of points' in a "lock box" to make sure you can get the points you have scored? Of course not! And if the bowling alley discovers you "foot faulted" and lowers your score back down by 5 points, does the bowling alley now have more score to give out? Of course not!

We all know how data entry works, but somehow this has gotten turned upside down and backwards by our politicians, media, and, most all, the prominent mainstream economists.

Just keep this in mind as a starting point: **The federal government doesn't ever "have" or "not have" any dollars.**

It's just like the stadium, which doesn't "have" or "not have" a hoard of points to give out. When it comes to the dollar, our government, working through its Federal agencies, the Federal Reserve Bank and the U.S. Treasury Department, is the score keeper. (And it also makes the rules!)

You now have the operational answer to the question: **"How are we going to pay for it?"** And the answer is: the same way government pays for anything, it changes the numbers in our bank accounts.

The federal government isn't going to "run out of money," as our President has mistakenly repeated. There is no such thing. Nor is it dependent on "getting" dollars from China or anywhere else. All it takes for the government to spend is for it to change the numbers up in bank accounts at its own bank, the Federal Reserve Bank. There is no numerical limit to how much money our government can spend, whenever it wants to spend. (This includes making interest payments, as well as Social Security and Medicare payments.) It encompasses all government payments made in dollars to anyone.

**This is not to say that excess government spending won't possibly cause prices to go up (which is inflation).** But it is to say that the government can't go broke and can't be bankrupt. There is simply no such thing.[1]

So why does no one in government seem to get it? Why does the Ways and Means Committee in Congress worry about "how we are going to pay for it?" It could be that they believe the popular notion that the federal government, just like any household, must somehow first "get" money to be able to spend it. Yes, they have heard that it's different for a government, but they don't quite believe it, and there's never a convincing explanation that makes sense to them.

---

[1] *I know you've got this question on your mind right now. I answer it a bit later in this book, but let me state the question and give you a quick answer to tide you over:*

**Question: If the government doesn't tax because it needs the money to spend, why tax at all?**

*Answer: The federal government taxes to regulate what economists call "aggregate demand" which is a fancy word for "spending power." In short, that means that if the economy is "too hot," then raising taxes will cool it down, and if it's "too cold," likewise, cutting taxes will warm it up. Taxes aren't about getting money to spend, they are about regulating our spending power to make sure we don't have too much and cause inflation, or too little which causes unemployment and recessions.*

What they all seem to miss is the difference between spending your own currency that only you create, and spending a currency someone else creates. To properly use this common federal government/household analogy in a meaningful way, we next look at an example of a "currency" created by a household.

The story begins with parents creating coupons they then use to pay their children for doing various household chores. Additionally, to "drive the model," the parents require the children to pay them a tax of 10 coupons a week to avoid punishment. This closely replicates taxation in the real economy, where we have to pay our taxes or face penalties. The coupons are now the new household currency. Think of the parents as "spending" these coupons to purchase "services" (chores) from their children. With this new household currency, the parents, like the federal government, are now the issuer of their own currency. And now you can see how a household with its own currency is indeed very much like a government with its own currency.

Let's begin by asking some questions about how this new household currency works. Do the parents have to somehow get coupons from their children before they can pay their coupons to their children to do chores? Of course not! In fact, the parents must first spend their coupons by paying their children to do household chores, to be able to collect the payment of 10 coupons a week from their children. How else can the children get the coupons they owe to their parents?

Likewise, in the real economy, the federal government, just like this household with its own coupons, doesn't have to get the dollars it spends from taxing or borrowing, or anywhere else, to be able to spend them. With modern technology, the federal government doesn't even have to print the dollars it spends the way the parents print their own coupons.

Remember, the federal government itself neither has nor doesn't have dollars, any more than the bowling alley ever has a box of points. When it comes to the dollar, our federal government is the scorekeeper. And how many coupons do the parents have in the parent/child coupon story? It doesn't matter. They could even just write down on a piece of paper how many coupons the children owe them, how many they have earned and how many they've paid each month. When the federal government spends, the funds don't "come from" anywhere any more than the points "come from" somewhere at the football stadium or the bowling alley. Nor does collecting taxes (or borrowing) somehow increase the government's "hoard of funds" available for spending.

In fact, the people at the U.S. Treasury who actually spend the money (by changing numbers on bank accounts up) don't even have the telephone numbers of - nor are they in contact with - the people at the IRS who collect taxes (they change the numbers on bank accounts down), or the other people at the U.S. Treasury who do the "borrowing" (issue the Treasury securities). If it mattered at all how much was taxed or borrowed to be able to spend, you'd think they at least would know each other's phone numbers! Clearly, it doesn't matter for their purposes.

From our point of view (not the federal government's), we need to first have U.S. dollars to be able to make payments. Just like the children need to earn the coupons from their parents before they can make their weekly coupon payments. And state governments, cities, and businesses are all in that same boat as well. They all need to be able to somehow get dollars before they can spend them. That could mean earning them, borrowing them, or selling something to get the dollars they need to be able to spend. In fact, as a point of logic, the dollars we need to pay taxes must, directly or indirectly, from the inception of the currency, come from government spending (or government lending, which I'll discuss later).

Now let's build a national currency from scratch. Imagine a new country with a newly announced currency. No one has any. Then the government proclaims, for example, that there will be a property tax. Well, how can it be paid? It can't, until after the government starts spending. Only after the government spends its new currency does the population have the funds to pay the tax.

To repeat: the funds to pay taxes, from inception, come from government spending (or lending). Where else can they come from?[2]

Yes, that means that the government has to spend first, to ultimately provide us with the funds we need to pay our taxes. The government, in this case, is just like the parents who have to spend their coupons first, before they can start actually collecting them from their children. And, neither the government, nor the parents, from inception, can collect more of their own currency than they spend. Where else could it possibly come from?[3]

---

[2] *For those of you who understand reserve accounting, note that the Fed can't do what's called a reserve drain without doing a reserve add. So what does the Fed do on settlement day when Treasury balances increase? It does repos - to add the funds to the banking system that banks then have to buy the Treasury Securities. Otherwise, the funds wouldn't be there to buy the Treasury securities, and the banks would have overdrafts in their reserve accounts. And what are overdrafts at the Fed? Functionally, an overdraft is a loan from the government. Ergo, one way or another, the funds used to buy the Treasury securities come from the government itself. Because the funds to pay taxes or buy government securities come from government spending, the government is best thought of as spending first, and then collecting taxes or borrowing later.*

[3] *Note on how this works inside the banking system: When you pay taxes by writing a check to the federal government, they debit your bank's reserve account at the Federal Reserve Bank reserves can only come from the Fed; the private sector can't generate them. If your bank doesn't have any, the check you write results in an overdraft in that bank's reserve account. An overdraft is a loan from the Fed. So in any case, the funds to make payments to the federal government can only come from the federal government.*

So while our politicians truly believe the government needs to take our dollars, either by taxing or borrowing, for them to be able to spend, the truth is:

**We need the federal government's spending to get the funds we need to pay our taxes.**

We don't get to change numbers, like the federal government does (or the bowling alley and the football stadium).[4] And just like the children who have to earn or somehow get their coupons to make their coupon payments, we have to earn or somehow get US dollars to make our tax payments. And, as you now understand, this is just like it happens in any household that issues its own coupons. The coupons the kids need to make their payments to their parents have to come from their parents.

And, as previously stated, government spending is in no case operationally constrained by revenues (tax payments and borrowings). Yes, there can be and there are "self-imposed" constraints on spending put there by Congress, but that's an entirely different matter. These include debt-ceiling rules, Treasury-overdraft rules, and restrictions of the Fed buying securities from the Treasury. They are all imposed by a Congress that does not have a working knowledge of the monetary system. And, with our current monetary arrangements, all of those self imposed constraints are counterproductive with regard to furthering public purpose.

---

[4] *Just a quick reminder that our state and local governments are users of the U.S. dollar, and not issuers, like the federal government is. In fact, the U.S. states are in a similar position as the rest of us: we both need to get funds into our bank accounts before we write our checks, or those checks will indeed bounce. In the parent/children analogy, we and the states are in much the same position as the children, who need to get first before they can give.*

All they do is put blockages in the monetary plumbing that wouldn't otherwise be there, and from time to time, create problems that wouldn't otherwise arise. In fact, it was some of these self-imposed blockages that caused the latest financial crisis to spill over to the real economy and contribute to the recession.

The fact that government spending is in no case operationally constrained by revenues means **there is no "solvency risk."** In other words, the federal government can always make any and all payments in its own currency, no matter how large the deficit is, or how few taxes it collects.

**This, however, does NOT mean that the government can spend all it wants without consequence. Over-spending can drive up prices and fuel inflation.**

What it does mean is that there is no solvency risk, which is to say that the federal government can't go broke, and there is no such thing as our government "running out of money to spend," as President Obama has incorrectly stated repeatedly.[5] Nor, as President Obama also stated, is U.S. government spending limited by what it can borrow.

So the next time you hear: "Where will the money for Social Security come from?" go ahead and tell them, "It's just data entry. It comes from the same place as your score at the bowling alley."

Putting it yet another way, U.S. government checks don't bounce, unless the government decides to bounce its own checks.

---

[5] *Quotes from President Barack Obama*

22

### Federal Government checks don't bounce.

A few years ago I gave a talk titled, "Government Checks Don't Bounce" in Australia at an economics conference. In the audience was the head of research for the Reserve Bank of Australia, Mr. David Gruen. It was high drama. I had been giving talks for several years to this group of academics, and I had not convinced most of them that government solvency wasn't an issue. They always started with the familiar, "What Americans don't understand is that it's different for a small, open economy like Australia than it is for the United States." There seemed to be no way to get it through their (perhaps) over-educated skulls that at least for this purpose, none of that matters. A spreadsheet is a spreadsheet. All but one Professor Bill Mitchell and a few of his colleagues seemed to have this mental block, and they deeply feared what would happen if the markets turned against Australia to somehow keep them from being able to "finance the deficit."

So I began my talk about how U.S. government checks don't bounce, and after a few minutes, David's hand shot up with the statement familiar to all modestly-advanced economic students: "If the interest rate on the debt is higher than the rate of growth of GDP, then the government's debt is unsustainable." This wasn't even presented as a question, but stated as a fact.

I then replied, "I'm an operations type of guy, David, so tell me, what do you mean by the word 'unsustainable'? Do you mean that if the interest rate is very high, and that in 20 years from now the government debt has grown to a large-enough number, the government won't be able to make its interest payments? And if it then writes a check to a pensioner, that that check will bounce?"

David got very quiet, deep in thought, thinking it through. "You know, when I came here, I didn't think I'd have to think through how the Reserve Bank's check-clearing works," he stated, in an attempt at humor. But no one in the room laughed or made a sound. They were totally focused on what his answer might be. It was a "showdown" on this issue. David finally said, "No, we'll clear the check, but it will cause inflation and the currency will go down. That's what people mean by unsustainable."

There was dead silence in the room. The long debate was over. Solvency is not an issue, even for a small, open economy. Bill and I instantly commanded an elevated level of respect, which took the usual outward form of "well of course, we always said that" from the former doubters and skeptics.

I continued with David, "Well, I think most pensioners are concerned about whether the funds will be there when they retire, and whether the Australian government will be able to pay them." To which David replied, "No, I think they are worried about inflation and the level of the Australian dollar." Then Professor Martin Watts, head of the Economics Department at the University of Newcastle inserted, "The Hell they are, David!" At that, David very thoughtfully conceded, "Yes, I suppose you're right."

So, what was actually confirmed to the Sydney academics in attendance that day? **Governments, using their own currency, can spend what they want, when they want, just like the football stadium can put points on the board at will. The consequences of overspending might be inflation or a falling currency, but never bounced checks.**

The fact is: government deficits can never cause a government to miss any size of payment. There is no solvency issue. There is no such thing as running out of money when spending is just changing numbers upwards in bank accounts at its own Federal Reserve Bank.

Yes, households, businesses, and even the states need to have dollars in their bank accounts when they write checks, or else those checks will bounce. That's because the dollars they spend are created by someone else - the federal government - and households, businesses, and the states are not the scorekeeper for the dollar.

## Why the Federal Government Taxes

So why then does the federal government tax us, if it doesn't actually get anything to spend or need to get anything to spend? (Hint: it's the same reason that the parents demand 10 coupons a week from their children, when the parents don't actually need the coupons for anything.)

There is a very good reason it taxes us. Taxes create an ongoing need in the economy to get dollars, and therefore an ongoing need for people to sell their goods and services and labor to get dollars. With tax liabilities in place, the government can buy things with its otherwise-worthless dollars, because someone needs the dollars to pay taxes. Just like the coupon tax on the children creates an ongoing need for the coupons, which can be earned by doing chores for the parents. Think of a property tax. (You're not ready to think about income taxes - it comes down to the same thing, but it's a lot more indirect and complicated). You have to pay the property tax in dollars or lose your house. It's just like the kids' situation, as they need to get 10 coupons or face the consequences. So now you are motivated to sell things - goods, services, your own labor - to get the dollars you need. It's just like the kids, who are motivated to do chores to get the coupons they need.

Finally, I have to connect the dots from some people needing dollars to pay their taxes to everyone wanting and using dollars for almost all of their buying and selling. To do that, let's go back to the example of a new country with a new currency, which I'll call "the crown," where the government levies a property tax. Let's assume the government levies this tax for the further purpose of raising an army, and offers jobs to soldiers who are paid in "crowns." Suddenly, a lot of people who own property now need to get crowns, and many of them won't want to get crowns directly from the government by serving as soldiers. So they start offering their goods and services for sale in exchange for the new crowns they need and want, hoping to get these crowns without having to join the army. Other people now see many things for sale they would like to have - chickens, corn, clothing and all kinds of services like haircuts, medical services and many other services. The sellers of these goods and services want to receive crowns to avoid having to join the army to get the money they need to pay their taxes. The fact that all these things are being offered for sale in exchange for crowns makes some other people join the army to get the money needed to buy some of those goods and services.

In fact, prices will adjust until as many soldiers as the government wants are enticed to join the army. Because until that happens, there won't be enough crowns spent by the government to allow the taxpayers to pay all of their taxes, and those needing the crowns, who don't want to go into the army, will cut the prices of their goods and services as much as they have to in order to get them sold, or else throw in the towel and join the army themselves.

The following is not merely a theoretical concept. It's exactly what happened in Africa in the 1800's, when the British established colonies there to grow crops. The British offered jobs to the local population, but none of them were interested in earning British coins. So the British placed a "hut tax" on all of their dwellings, payable only in British coins. Suddenly, the area was "monetized," as everyone now needed British coins, and the local population started offering things for sale, as well as their labor, to get the needed coins. The British could then hire them and pay them in British coins to work the fields and grow their crops.

This is exactly what the parents did to get labor hours from their children to get the chores done. And that's exactly how what are called "non convertible currencies" work (no more gold standards and very few fixed exchange rates are left), like the U.S. dollar, Japanese yen, and British pound.

Now we're ready to look at the role of taxes from a different angle, that of today's economy, using the language of economics. A learned economist today would say that "taxes function to reduce aggregate demand." Their term, "aggregate demand," is just a fancy term for "spending power."

The government taxes us and takes away our money for one reason - so we have that much less to spend which makes the currency that much more scarce and valuable. Taking away our money can also be thought of as leaving room for the government to spend without causing inflation. Think of the economy as one big department store full of all the goods and services we all produce and offer for sale every year. We all get paid enough in wages and profits to buy everything in that store, assuming we would spend all the money we earn and all the profits we make. (And if we borrow to spend, we can buy even more than there is in that store.) But when some of our money goes to pay taxes, we are left short of the spending power we need to buy all of what's for sale in the store. This gives government the "room" to buy what it wants so that when it spends what it wants, the combined spending of government and the rest of us isn't too much for what's for sale in the store.

However, when the government taxes too much - relative to its spending - total spending isn't enough to make sure everything in the store gets sold. When businesses can't sell all that they produce, people lose their jobs and have even less money to spend, so even less gets sold. Then more people lose their jobs, and the economy goes into a downward spiral we call a recession.

Keep in mind that the public purpose behind government doing all this is to provide a public infrastructure. This includes the military, the legal system, the legislature and the executive branch of government, etc. So there is quite a bit that even the most conservative voters would have the government do.

So I look at it this way: for the "right" amount of government spending, which we presume is necessary to run the nation the way we would like to see it run, how high should taxes be? The reason I look at it this way is because the "right amount of government spending" is an economic and political decision that, properly understood, has nothing to do with government finances. The real "costs" of running the government are the real goods and services it consumes - all the labor hours, fuel, electricity, steel, carbon fiber, hard drives, etc. that would otherwise be available for the private sector. So when the government takes those real resources for its own purposes, there are that many fewer real resources left for private-sector activity. For example, the real cost of the "right-size" army with enough soldiers for defense is that there are fewer workers left in the private sector to grow the food, build the cars, do the doctoring and nursing and administrative tasks, sell us stocks and real estate, paint our houses, mow our lawns, etc. etc. etc.

Therefore, the way I see it, we first set the size of government at the "right" level of public infrastructure, based on real benefits and real costs, and not the "financial" considerations. The monetary system is then the tool we use to achieve our real economic and political objectives, and not the source of information as to what those objectives are. Then, after deciding what we need to spend to have the right-sized government, we adjust taxes so that we all have enough spending power to buy what's still for sale in the "store" after the government is done with its shopping. In general, I'd expect taxes to be quite a bit lower than government spending, for reasons already explained and also expanded on later in this book. In fact, a budget deficit of perhaps 5% of our gross domestic product might turn out to be the norm, which in today's economy is about $750 billion annually. However, that number by itself is of no particular economic consequence, and could be a lot higher or a lot lower, depending on the circumstances. What matters is that the purpose of taxes is to balance the economy and make sure it's not too hot nor too cold. And federal government spending is set at this right amount, given the size and scope of government we want.

That means we should NOT grow the size of government to help the economy out of a slowdown. We should already be at the right size for government, and therefore not add to it every time the economy slows down. So while increasing government spending during a slowdown will indeed make the numbers work, and will end the recession, for me that is far less desirable than accomplishing the same thing with the right tax cuts in sufficient-enough size to restore private-sector spending to the desired amounts.

Even worse is increasing the size of government just because the government might find itself with a surplus. Again, government finances tell us nothing about how large the government *should* be. That decision is totally independent of government finances. The right amount of government spending has nothing to do with tax revenues or the ability to borrow, as both of those are only tools for implementing policy on behalf of public purpose, and not reasons for spending or not spending, and not sources of revenue needed for actual government spending.

I'll get specific on what role I see for government later in this book, but rest assured, my vision is for a far more streamlined and efficient government, one that is intensely focused on the basics of fundamental public purpose. Fortunately, there are readily available and infinitely sensible ways to do this. We can put the right incentives in place which channel market forces with guidance to better promote the public purpose with far less regulation. This will result in a government and culture that will continue to be the envy of the world. It will be a government that expresses our American values of rewarding hard work and innovation, and promoting equal opportunity, equitable outcomes and enforceable laws and regulations we can respect with true pride.

But I digress. Returning to the issue of how high taxes need to be, recall that if the government simply tried to buy what it wanted to buy and didn't take away any of our spending power, there would be no taxes - it would be "too much money chasing too few goods," with the result being inflation. In fact, with no taxes, nothing would even be offered for sale in exchange for the government money in the first place, as previously discussed.

To prevent the government's spending from causing that kind of inflation, the government must take away some of our spending power by taxing us, not to actually pay for anything, but so that their spending won't cause inflation. An economist would say it this way: taxes function to regulate aggregate demand, not to raise revenue per se. In other words, the government taxes us, and takes away our money, to prevent inflation, not to actually get our money in order to spend it.

Restated one more time: **Taxes function to regulate the economy, and not to get money for Congress to spend**.

And, again, the government neither has nor doesn't have dollars; it simply changes numbers in our bank accounts upward when it spends and downwards when it taxes. All of this is, presumably, for the public purpose of regulating the economy.

But as long as government continues to believe this first of the seven deadly innocent frauds, that they need to get money from taxing or borrowing in order to spend, they will continue to support policies that constrain output and employment and prevent us from achieving what are otherwise readily-available economic outcomes.

### *Deadly Innocent Fraud #2:*
With government deficits, we are leaving our debt burden to our children.

### *Fact:*
Collectively, in real terms, there is no such burden possible. Debt or no debt, our children get to consume whatever they can produce.

This deadly innocent fraud is often the first answer most people give to what they perceive to be the main problem associated with government deficit spending. Borrowing now means paying for today's spending later. Or, as commonly seen and heard in the media:

**"Higher deficits today mean higher taxes tomorrow."**

And paying later means that somehow our children's real standard of living and general well-being will be lowered in the future because of our deficit spending now.

Professional economists call this the "intergenerational" debt issue. It is thought that if the federal government deficit spends, it is somehow leaving the real burden of today's expenditures to be paid for by future generations.

And the numbers are staggering!

But, fortunately, like all of the seven deadly innocent frauds, it is all readily dismissed in a way that can be easily understood. In fact, the idea of our children being somehow necessarily deprived of real goods and services in the future because of what's called the national debt is nothing less than ridiculous.

Here's a story that illustrates the point. Several years ago, I ran into former Senator and Governor of Connecticut, Lowell Weicker, and his wife Claudia on a boat dock in St. Croix. I asked Governor Weicker what was wrong with the country's fiscal policy. He replied we have to stop running up these deficits and leaving the burden of paying for today's spending to our children.

So I then asked him the following questions to hopefully illustrate the hidden flaw in his logic: "When our children build 15 million cars per year 20 years from now, will they have to send them back in time to 2008 to pay off their debt? Are we still sending real goods and services back in time to 1945 to pay off the lingering debt from World War II?"

And today, as I run for the U.S. Senate in Connecticut, nothing has changed. The ongoing theme of the other candidates is that we are borrowing from the likes of China to pay for today's spending and leaving our children and grandchildren to pay the bill.

Of course, we all know we don't send real goods and services back in time to pay off federal government deficits, and that our children won't have to do that either.

Nor is there any reason government spending from previous years should prevent our children from going to work and producing all the goods and services they are capable of producing. And in our children's future, just like today, whoever is alive will be able to go to work and produce and consume their real output of goods and services, no matter how many U.S. Treasury securities are outstanding. There is no such thing as giving up current-year output to the past, and sending it back in time to previous generations. Our children won't and can't pay us back for anything we leave them, even if they wanted to.

Nor is the financing of deficit spending anything of any consequence. When government spends, it just changes numbers up in our bank accounts. More specifically, all the commercial banks we use for our banking have bank accounts at the Fed called reserve accounts. Foreign governments have reserve accounts at the Fed as well. These reserve accounts at the Fed are just like checking accounts at any other bank.

When government spends without taxing, all it does is change the numbers up in the appropriate checking account (reserve account) at the Fed. This means that when the government makes a $2,000 Social Security payment to you, for example, it changes the number up in your bank's checking account at the Fed by $2,000, which also automatically changes the number up in your account at your bank by $2,000.

Next, you need to know what a U.S. Treasury security actually is. A U.S. Treasury security is nothing more than a savings account at the Fed. When you buy a Treasury security, you send your dollars to the Fed and then some time in the future, they send the dollars back plus interest. The same holds true for any savings account at any bank. You send the bank dollars and you get them back plus interest. Let's say that your bank decides to buy $2,000 worth of Treasury securities. To pay for those Treasury securities, the Fed reduces the number of dollars that your bank has in its checking account at the Fed by $2,000 and adds $2,000 to your bank's savings account at the Fed. (I'm calling the Treasury securities "savings accounts," which is all they are.)

In other words, when the U.S. government does what's called "borrowing money," all it does is move funds from checking accounts at the Fed to savings accounts (Treasury securities) at the Fed. In fact, the entire $13 trillion national debt is nothing more than the economy's total holdings of savings accounts at the Fed.

And what happens when the Treasury securities come due, and that "debt" has to be paid back? Yes, you guessed it, the Fed merely shifts the dollar balances from the savings accounts (Treasury securities) at the Fed to the appropriate checking accounts at the Fed (reserve accounts). Nor is this anything new. It's been done exactly like this for a very long time, and no one seems to understand how simple it is and that it never will be a problem.

## Federal Government Taxing and Spending Does Influence Distribution

Distribution is about who gets all the goods and services that are produced. In fact, this is what politicians do every time they pass legislation. They re-direct real goods and services by decree, for better or worse. And the odds of doing it for better are substantially decreased when they don't understand the Seven Deadly Innocent Frauds. Each year, for example, Congress discusses tax policy, always with an eye to the distribution of income and spending. Many seek to tax those "who can most afford it" and direct federal spending to "those in need." And they also decide how to tax interest, capital gains, estates, etc. as well as how to tax income. All of these are distributional issues.

In addition, Congress decides who the government hires and fires, who it buys things from, and who gets direct payments. Congress also makes laws that directly affect many other aspects of prices and incomes.

Foreigners who hold U.S. dollars are particularly at risk. They earn those dollars from selling us real goods and services, yet they have no assurance that they will be able to buy real goods and services from us in the future. Prices could go up (inflation) and the U.S. government could legally impose all kinds of taxes on anything foreigners wish to buy from us, which reduces their spending power.

Think of all those cars Japan sold to us for under $2,000 years ago. They've been holding those dollars in their savings accounts at the Fed (they own U.S. Treasury securities), and if they now would want to spend those dollars, they would probably have to pay in excess of $20,000 per car to buy cars from us. What can they do about the higher prices? Call the manager and complain? They've traded millions of perfectly good cars to us in exchange for credit balances on the Fed's books that can buy only what

34

we allow them to buy. And look at what happened recently - the Federal Reserve cut rates, which reduced the interest Japan earns on its U.S.-Treasury securities. (This discussion continues in a subsequent innocent fraud.)

This is all perfectly legal and business as usual, as each year's output is "divided up" among the living. None of the real output gets "thrown away" because of outstanding debt, no matter how large. Nor does outstanding debt reduce output and employment, except of course when ill-informed policymakers decide to take anti-deficit measures that do reduce output and employment. Unfortunately, that is currently the case, and that is why this is a deadly innocent fraud.

Today (April 15, 2010), it's clear that Congress is taking more spending power away from us in taxes than is needed to make room for their own spending. Even after we spend what we want and the government does all of its massive spending, there's still a lot left unsold in that big department store called the economy.

How do we know that? Easy! Count the bodies in the unemployment lines. Look at the massive amount of excess capacity in the economy. Look at what the Fed calls the "output gap," which is the difference between what we could produce at full employment and what we are now producing. It's enormous.

Sure, there's a record deficit and national debt, which, you now know, means that we all have that much in savings accounts at the Fed called Treasury securities. Incidentally, the cumulative U.S. budget deficit, adjusted for the size of the economy, is still far below Japan's, far below most of Europe and very far below the World War II U.S. deficits that got us out of the Depression (with no debt burden consequences).

If you've gotten this far into this book you may already know why the size of the deficit isn't a financial issue. So hopefully, you know that taxes function to regulate the economy, and not to raise revenue, as Congress thinks. When I look at today's economy, it's screaming at me that the problem is that people don't have enough money to spend. It's not telling me they have too much spending power and are over-spending. Who would not agree?

Unemployment has doubled and GDP is more than 10% below where it would be if Congress wasn't over-taxing us and taking so much spending power away from us.

When we operate at less than our potential - at less than full employment - then we are depriving our children of the real goods and services we could be producing on their behalf. Likewise, when we cut back on our support of higher education, we are depriving our children of the knowledge they'll need to be the very best they can be in their future. So also, when we cut back on basic research and space exploration, we are depriving our children of all the fruits of that labor that instead we are transferring to the unemployment lines.

So yes, those alive get to consume this year's output, and also get to decide to use some of the output as "investment goods and services," which should increase future output. And yes, Congress has a big say in who consumes this year's output. Potential distributional issues due to previous federal deficits can be readily addressed by Congress and distribution can be legally altered to their satisfaction.

## So How Do We Pay Off China?

Those worried about paying off the national debt can't possibly understand how it all works at the operational, nuts and bolts (debits and credits) level. Otherwise they would realize that question is entirely inapplicable. What they don't understand is that both dollars and U.S. Treasury debt (securities) are nothing more than "accounts," which are nothing more than numbers that the government makes on its own books.

So let's start by looking at how we got to where we are today with China. It all started when China wanted to sell things to us and we wanted to buy them. For example, let's suppose that the U.S. Army wanted to buy $1 billion worth of uniforms from China, and China wanted to sell $1 billion worth of uniforms to the U.S. Army at that price. So the Army buys $1 billion worth of uniforms from China. First, understand that both parties are happy. There is no "imbalance." China would rather have the 1 billion U.S. dollars than the uniforms or they wouldn't have sold them, and the U.S. Army would rather have the uniforms than the money or it wouldn't have bought them. The transactions are all voluntary, and all in U.S. dollars. But back to our point - how does China get paid?

China has a reserve account at the Federal Reserve Bank. To quickly review, a reserve account is nothing more than a fancy name for a checking account. It's the Federal Reserve Bank so they call it a reserve account instead of a checking account. To pay China, the Fed adds 1 billion U.S. dollars to China's checking account at the Fed. It does this by changing the numbers in China's checking account up by 1 billion U.S. dollars. The numbers don't come from anywhere any more than the numbers on a scoreboard at a football come from anywhere. China then has some choices. It can do nothing and keep the $1 billion in its checking account at the Fed, or it can buy U.S. Treasury securities.

Again, to quickly review, a U.S. Treasury security is nothing more than a fancy name for a savings account at the Fed. The buyer gives the Fed money, and gets it back later with interest. That's what a savings account is - you give a bank money and you get it back later with interest.

So let's say China buys a one-year Treasury security. All that happens is that the Fed subtracts $1 billion from China's checking account at the Fed, and adds $1 billion to China's savings account at the Fed. And all that happens a year later when China's one-year Treasury bill comes due is that the Fed removes this money from China's savings account at the Fed (including interest) and adds it to China's checking account at the Fed.

Right now, China is holding some $2 trillion of U.S. Treasury securities. So what do we do when they mature and it's time to pay China back? We remove those dollars from their savings account at the Fed and add them to their checking account at the Fed, and wait for them to say what, if anything, they might want to do next.

This is what happens when all U.S. government debt comes due, which happens continuously. The Fed removes dollars from savings accounts and adds dollars to checking accounts on its books. When people buy Treasury securities, the Fed removes dollars from their checking accounts and adds them to their savings accounts. So what's all the fuss?

It's all a tragic misunderstanding.

China knows we don't need them for "financing our deficits" and is playing us for fools. Today, that includes Geithner, Clinton, Obama, Summers and the rest of the administration. It also includes Congress and the media.

Now let me describe this all in a more technical manner for those of you who may be interested. When a Treasury bill, note or bond is purchased by a bank, for example, the government makes two entries on its spreadsheet that we call the "monetary system." First, it debits (subtracts from) the buyer's reserve account (checking account) at the Fed. Then it increases (credits) the buyer's securities account (savings account) at the Fed. As before, the government simply changes numbers on its own spreadsheet - one number gets changed down and another gets changed up. And when the dreaded day arrives, and the Treasury securities which China holds come due and need to be repaid, the Fed again simply changes two numbers on its own spreadsheet. The Fed debits (subtracts from) China's securities account at the Fed. And then it credits (adds to) China's reserve (checking) account at the Fed. That's all - debt paid!

China now has its money back. It has a (very large) U.S.-dollar balance in its checking account at the Fed. If it wants anything else - cars, boats, real estate, other currencies - it has to buy them at market prices from a willing seller who wants dollar deposits in return. And if China does buy something, the Fed will subtract that amount from China's checking account and add that amount to the checking account of whomever China bought it all from.

Notice too, that "paying off China" doesn't change China's stated $U.S. wealth. They simply have dollars in a checking account rather than U.S. Treasury securities (a savings account) of equal dollars. And if they want more Treasury securities instead, no problem, the Fed just moves their U.S. dollars from their checking account to their savings account again, by appropriately changing the numbers.

Paying off the entire U.S. national debt is but a matter of subtracting the value of the maturing securities from one account at the Fed, and adding that value to another account at the Fed. These transfers are non-events for the real economy and not the source of dire stress presumed by mainstream economists, politicians, businesspeople, and the media.

One more time: to pay off the national debt the government changes two entries in its own spreadsheet - a number that says how many securities are owned by the private sector is changed down and another number that says how many U.S. dollars are being kept at the Fed in reserve accounts is changed up. Nothing more. Debt paid. All creditors have their money back. What's the big deal?

So what happens if China refuses to buy our debt at current low-interest rates paid to them? Interest rates have to go up to attract their purchase of the Treasury Securities, right? Wrong!

They can leave it in their checking account. It's of no consequence to a government that understands its own monetary system. The funds are not used for spending, as previously described. There are no negative consequences of funds being in a checking account at the Fed rather than a savings account at the Fed.

What happens if China says, "We don't want to keep a checking account at the Fed anymore. Pay us in gold or some other means of exchange!" They simply do not have this option under our current "fiat currency" system[6] as they would have known when they sold the uniforms to the U.S. Army and had the money put into their checking account at the Fed. If they want something other than dollars, they have to buy it from a willing seller, just like the rest of us do when we spend our dollars.

Some day it will be our children changing numbers on what will be their spreadsheet, just as seamlessly as we did, and our parents did, though hopefully with a better understanding! But for now, the deadly innocent fraud of leaving the national debt to our children continues to drive policy, and keeps us from optimizing output and employment.

The lost output and depreciated human capital is the real price we and our children are paying now that diminishes both the present and the future. We make do with less than what we can produce and sustain high levels of unemployment (along with all the associated crime, family problems and medical issues) while our children are deprived of the real investments that would have been made on their behalf if we knew how to keep our human resources fully employed and productive.

---

[6] *In 1971, the US went off the gold standard for international accounts, formally ending all government-guaranteed convertibility of the U.S. dollar.*

### *Deadly Innocent Fraud #3:*
Federal Government budget deficits take away savings.

### *Fact:*
Federal Government budget deficits ADD to savings.

### Lawrence Summers

Several years ago I had a meeting with Senator Tom Daschle and then-Assistant Treasury Secretary Lawrence Summers. I had been discussing these innocent frauds with the Senator, and explaining how they were working against the well-being of those who voted for him. So he set up this meeting with the Assistant Treasury Secretary, who is also a former Harvard economics professor and has two uncles who have won Nobel prizes in economics, to get his response and hopefully confirm what I was saying.

I opened with a question: "Larry, what's wrong with the budget deficit?" He replied: "It takes away savings that could be used for investment." I then objected: "No it doesn't, all Treasury securities do is offset operating factors at the Fed. It has nothing to do with savings and investment." To which he retorted: "Well, I really don't understand reserve accounting, so I can't discuss it at that level."

Senator Daschle was looking on at all this in disbelief. This Harvard professor of economics, Assistant Treasury Secretary Lawrence Summers didn't understand reserve accounting? Sad but true.

So I spent the next twenty minutes explaining the "paradox of thrift" (more detail on this innocent fraud #6 later) step by step, which he sort of got right when he finally responded: "...so we need more investment which will show up as savings?" I responded with a friendly "yes," after giving this first year economics lesson to the good Harvard professor, and ended the meeting. The next day, I saw him on a podium with the Concord Coalition - a band of deficit terrorists - talking about the grave dangers of the budget deficit.

This third deadly innocent fraud is alive and well at the very highest levels. So here's how it really works, and it could not be simpler: Any $U.S. government deficit exactly EQUALS the total net increase in the holdings ($U.S. financial assets) of the rest of us - businesses and households, residents and non residents - what is called the "non government" sector.
In other words, government deficits equal increased "monetary savings" for the rest of us, to the penny.

Simply put, government deficits ADD to our savings (to the penny). This is an accounting fact, not theory or philosophy. There is no dispute. It is basic national income accounting. For example, if the government deficit last year was $1 trillion, it means that the net increase in savings of financial assets for everyone else combined was exactly, to the penny, $1 trillion. (For those who took some economics courses, you might remember that net savings of financial assets is held as some combination of actual cash, Treasury securities and member bank deposits at the Federal Reserve.) This is Economics 101 and first year money banking. It is beyond dispute. It's an accounting identity. Yet it's misrepresented continuously, and at the highest levels of political authority. They are just plain wrong.

Just ask anyone at the CBO (Congressional Budget Office), as I have, and they will tell you they must "balance the checkbook" and make sure the government deficit equals our new savings, or they would have to stay late and find their accounting mistake.

As before, it's just a bunch of spreadsheet entries on the government's own spreadsheet. When the accountants debit (subtract from) the account called "government" when government spends, they also credit (add to) the accounts of whoever gets those funds. When the government account goes down, some other account goes up, by exactly the same amount.

Next is an example of how, operationally, government deficits add to savings. This also puts to rest a ridiculous new take on this innocent fraud that's popped up recently:

"Deficit spending means the government borrows from one person and gives it to another, so nothing new is added - it's just a shift of money from one person to another." In other words, they are saying that deficits don't add to our savings, but just shift savings around. This could not be more wrong! So let's demonstrate how deficits do ADD to savings, and not just shift savings:

1. Start with the government selling $100 billion in Treasury securities. (Note: this sale is voluntary, which means that the buyer buys the securities because he wants to. Presumably, he believes that he is better off buying them than not buying them. No one is ever forced to buy government securities. They get sold at auction to the highest bidder who is willing to accept the lowest yield.)

2. When the buyers of these securities pay for them, checking accounts at the Fed are reduced by $100 billion to make the payment. In other words, money in checking accounts at the Fed is exchanged for the new Treasury securities, which are savings accounts at the Fed. At this point, non-government savings is unchanged. The buyers now have their new Treasury securities as savings, rather than the money that was in their checking accounts before they bought the Treasury securities.

3. Now the Treasury spends $100 billion after the sale of the $100 billion of new Treasury securities, on the usual things government spends its money on.

4. This Treasury spending adds back $100 billion to someone's checking accounts.

5. The non-government sector now has its $100 billion of checking accounts back AND it has the $100 billion of new Treasury securities.

Bottom line: the deficit spending of $100 billion directly added $100 billion of savings in the form of new Treasury securities to non-government savings (non-government means everyone but the government).

The savings of the buyer of the $100 billion of new Treasury securities shifted from money in his checking account to his holdings of the Treasury securities (savings accounts).    Then when the Treasury spent $100 billion after selling the Treasury securities, the savings of recipients of that $100 billion of spending saw their checking accounts increase by that amount.

So, to the original point, deficit spending doesn't just shift financial assets (U.S. dollars and Treasury securities) outside of the government. Instead, deficit spending directly adds exactly that amount of savings of financial assets to the non-government sector. And likewise, a federal budget surplus directly subtracts exactly that much from our savings. And the media and politicians and even top economists all have it BACKWARDS!

In July 1999, the front page of the Wall Street Journal had two headlines. Towards the left was a headline praising President Clinton and the record government budget surplus, and explaining how well fiscal policy was working. On the right margin was a headline stating that Americans weren't saving enough and we would have to work harder to save more. Then a few pages later, there was a graph with one line showing the surplus going up, and another line showing savings going down. They were nearly identical, but going in opposite directions, and clearly showing the gains in the government surplus roughly equaled the losses in private savings.

There can't be a budget surplus with private savings increasing (including non-resident savings of $U.S. financial assets). There is no such thing, yet not a single mainstream economist or government official had it right.

### Al Gore

Early in 2000, in a private home in Boca Raton, FL, I was seated next to then-Presidential Candidate Al Gore at a fundraiser/dinner to discuss the economy. The first thing he asked was how I thought the next president should spend the coming $5.6 trillion surplus that was forecasted for the next 10 years. I explained that there wasn't going to be a $5.6 trillion surplus, because that would mean a $5.6 trillion drop in non-government savings of financial assets, which was a ridiculous proposition. At the time, the private sector didn't even have that much in savings to be taxed away by the government, and the latest surplus of several hundred billion dollars had already removed more than enough private savings to turn the Clinton boom into the soon-to-come bust.

I pointed out to Candidate Gore that the last six periods of surplus in our more than two hundred-year history had been followed by the only six depressions in our history. Also, I mentioned that the coming bust would be due to allowing the budget to go into surplus and drain our savings, resulting in a recession that would not end until the deficit got high enough to add back our lost income and savings and deliver the aggregate demand needed to restore output and employment. I suggested that the $5.6 trillion surplus which was forecasted for the next decade would more likely be a $5.6 trillion deficit, as normal savings desires are likely to average 5% of GDP over that period of time.

That is pretty much what happened. The economy fell apart, and President Bush temporarily reversed it with his massive deficit spending in 2003. But after that, and before we had had enough deficit spending to replace the financial assets lost to the Clinton surplus years (a budget surplus takes away exactly that much savings from the rest of us), we let the deficit get too small again. And after the sub-prime debt-driven bubble burst, we again fell apart due to a deficit that was and remains far too small for the circumstances.

For the current level of government spending, we are being over-taxed and we don't have enough after-tax income to buy what's for sale in that big department store called the economy.

Anyway, Al was a good student, went over all the details, agreeing that it made sense and was indeed what might happen. However, he said he couldn't "go there." I told him that I understood the political realities, as he got up and gave his talk about how he was going to spend the coming surpluses.

### Robert Rubin

Ten years ago, around the year 2000 just before it all fell apart, I found myself in a private client meeting at Citibank with Robert Rubin, former U.S. Treasury Secretary under President Clinton, and about 20 Citibank clients. Mr. Rubin gave his take on the economy and indicated that the low savings rate might turn out to be a problem. With just a few minutes left, I told him I agreed about the low savings rate being an issue and added, "Bob, does anyone in Washington realize that the budget surplus takes away savings from the non-government sectors?" He replied, "No, the surplus adds to savings. When the government runs a surplus, it buys

Treasury securities in the market, and that adds to savings and investment." To that I responded, "No, when we run a surplus, we have to sell our securities to the Fed (cash in our savings accounts at the Fed) to get the money to pay our taxes, and our net financial assets and savings go down by the amount of the surplus." Rubin stated, "No, I think you're wrong." I let it go and the meeting was over. My question was answered. If he didn't understand surpluses removed savings, then no one in the Clinton administration did. And the economy crashed soon afterwards.

When the January 2009 savings report was released, and the press noted that the rise in savings to 5% of GDP was the highest since 1995, they failed to note the current budget deficit passed 5% of GDP, which also happens to be the highest it's been since 1995.

Clearly, the mainstream doesn't yet realize that deficits add to savings. And if Al Gore does, he isn't saying anything. So watch this year as the federal deficit goes up and savings, too, goes up. Again, the only source of "net $U.S. monetary savings" (financial assets) for the non-government sectors combined (both residents and non-residents) is U.S. government deficit spending.

But watch how the very people who want us to save more, at the same time want to "balance the budget" by taking away our savings, either through spending cuts or tax increases. They are all talking out of both sides of their mouths. They are part of the problem, not part of the solution. And they are at the very highest levels.

Except for one.


### Professor Wynne Godley

Professor Wynne Godley, retired head of Economics at Cambridge University and now over 80 years old, was widely renowned as the most successful forecaster of the

British economy for multiple decades. And he did it all with his "sector analysis," which had at its core the fact that the government deficit equals the savings of financial assets of the other sectors combined. However, even with the success of his forecasting, the iron-clad support from the pure accounting facts, and the weight of his office (all of which continues to this day), he has yet to convince the mainstream of the validity of his teachings.

So now we know:

- Federal deficits are not the "awful things" that the mainstream believes them to be. Yes, deficits do matter. Excess spending can cause inflation. But the government isn't going to go broke.
- Federal deficits won't burden our children.
- Federal deficits don't just shift funds from one person to another.
- Federal deficits add to our savings.

So what is the role of deficits in regard to policy? It's very simple. Whenever spending falls short of sustaining our output and employment, when we don't have enough spending power to buy what's for sale in that big department store we call the economy, government can act to make sure that our own output is sold by either cutting taxes or increasing government spending.

Taxes function to regulate our spending power and the economy in general. If the "right" level of taxation needed to support output and employment happens to be a lot less than government spending, that resulting budget deficit is nothing to be afraid of regarding solvency, sustainability, or doing bad by our children.

If people want to work and earn money but don't want to spend it, fine! Government can either keep cutting taxes until we decide to spend and buy our own output, and/or buy the output (award contracts for infrastructure repairs, national security, medical research, and the like). The choices are political. The right-sized deficit is the one that gets us to where we want to be with regards to output and employment, as well as the size of government we want, no matter how large or how small a deficit that might be.

What matters is the real life - output and employment - size of the deficit, which is an accounting statistic. In the 1940's, an economist named Abba Lerner called this, "Functional Finance," and wrote a book by that name (which is still very relevant today).

### Deadly Innocent Fraud #4:
Social Security is broken.

### Fact:
Federal Government Checks Don't Bounce.

If there is one thing that all members of Congress believe, it's that Social Security is broken. President (elect) Obama has said "the money won't be there," President Bush used the word "bankruptcy" four times in one day and Senator McCain often claims that Social Security is broken. They are all wrong.

As we've already discussed, the government never has or doesn't have any of its own money. It spends by changing numbers in our bank accounts. This includes Social Security. There is no operational constraint on the government's ability to meet all Social Security payments in a timely manner. It doesn't matter what the numbers are in the Social Security Trust Fund account, because the trust fund is nothing more than record-keeping, as are all accounts at the Fed.

When it comes time to make Social Security payments, all the government has to do is change numbers up in the beneficiary's accounts, and then change numbers down in the trust fund accounts to keep track of what it did. If the trust fund number goes negative, so be it. That just reflects the numbers that are changed up as payments to beneficiaries are made.

One of the major discussions in Washington is whether or not to privatize Social Security. As you might be guessing by now, that entire discussion makes no sense whatsoever, so let me begin with that and then move on.

What is meant by the privatization of Social Security, and what effect does that have on the economy and you as an individual?

The idea of privatization is that:
1. Social Security taxes and benefits are reduced.
2. The amount of the tax reduction is used to buy specified shares of stock.
3. Because the government is going to collect that much less in taxes, the budget deficit will be that much higher, and so the government will have to sell that many more Treasury securities to "pay for it all" (as they say).

Got it? In simpler words:
- You have less taken out of your paycheck for Social Security each week.
- You get to use the funds they no longer take from you to buy stocks.
- You later will collect a bit less in Social Security payments when you retire.
- You will own stocks which will hopefully become worth more than the Social Security payments that you gave up.

From the point of view of the individual, it looks like an interesting trade-off. The stocks you buy only have to go up modestly over time for you to be quite a bit ahead.

Those who favor this plan say yes, it's a relatively large one-time addition to the deficit, but the savings in Social Security payments down the road for the government pretty much makes up for that, and the payments going into the stock market will help the economy grow and prosper.

Those against the proposal say the stock market is too risky for this type of thing and point to the large drop in 2008 as an example. And if people lose in the stock market, the government will be compelled to increase Social Security retirement payments to keep retirees out of poverty.

Therefore, unless we want to risk a high percentage of our seniors falling below the poverty line, the government will be taking all the risk.

They are both terribly mistaken. (Who would have thought!)

The major flaw in this mainstream dialogue is what is called a "fallacy of composition." The typical textbook example of a fallacy of composition is the football game where you can see better if you stand up, and then conclude that everyone would see better if everyone stood up. Wrong! If everyone stands up, then no one can see better, and all are worse off. They all are looking at the micro level, which is individual Social Security participants, rather than looking at the macro level, the entire population.

To understand what's fundamentally wrong at the macro (big picture, top down) level, you first have to understand that participating in Social Security is functionally the same as buying a government bond. Let me explain. With the current Social Security program, you give the government your dollars now, and it gives you back dollars later. This is exactly what happens when you buy a government bond (or put your money in a savings account). You give the government your dollars now and you get dollars back later plus any interest. Yes, one might turn out to be a better investment and give you a higher return, but apart from the rate of return, they are very much the same. (Now that you know this, you are way ahead of Congress, by the way.)

### Steve Moore

Now you are ready to read about the conversation I had several years back with Steve Moore, then head of economics at the CATO institute, now a CNBC regular and a long-time supporter of privatizing Social Security. Steve came down to Florida to speak about Social Security at one of my conferences. He gave a talk that called for letting people put their money in the stock market rather than making Social Security payments, contending that they will be better off over time when they retire. Also, he argued that a one-time increase in the government budget deficit will be both well worth it and probably "paid down" over time in the expansion to follow, as all that money going into stocks will help the economy grow and prosper.

At that point I led off the question and answer session.

Warren: "Steve, giving the government your money now in the form of Social Security taxes and getting it back later, is functionally the same as buying a government bond, where you give the government money now, and it gives it back to you later. The only difference is the return that seniors will get."

Steve: "OK, but with government bonds, you get a higher return than with Social Security, which only pays your money back at 2% interest. Social Security is a bad investment for individuals."

Warren: "OK, I'll get to the investment aspect later, but let me continue. Under your privatization proposal, the government would reduce Social Security payments and the employees would put that money into the stock market."

Steve: "Yes, about $100 per month, and only into approved, high quality stocks."

Warren: "OK and the U.S. Treasury would have to issue and sell additional securities to cover the reduced revenues."

Steve: "Yes, and it would also be reducing Social Security payments down the road."

Warren: "Right. So to continue with my point, the employees buying the stock buy them from someone else, so all the stocks do is change hands. No new money goes into the economy."

Steve: "Right."

Warren: "And the people who sold the stock then have the money from the sale which is the money that buys the government bonds."

Steve: "Yes, you can think of it that way."

Warren: "So what has happened is that the employees stopped buying into Social Security, which we agree was functionally the same as buying a government bond, and instead they bought stocks. And other people sold their stocks and bought the newly-issued government bonds. So looking at it from the macro level, all that happened is that some stocks changed hands and some bonds changed hands. Total stocks outstanding and total bonds outstanding, if you count Social Security as a bond, remained about the same. And so this should have no influence on the economy or total savings, or anything else apart from generating transactions costs?"

Steve: "Yes, I suppose you can look at it that way, but I look at it as privatizing, and I believe people can invest their money better than government can."

Warren: "Ok, but you agree that the amount of stocks held by the public hasn't changed, so with this proposal, nothing changes for the economy as a whole."

Steve: "But it does change things for Social Security participants."

Warren: "Yes, with exactly the opposite change for others. And none of this has even been discussed by Congress or any mainstream economist? It seems you have an ideological bias toward privatization rhetoric, rather than the substance of the proposal."

Steve: "I like it because I believe in privatization. I believe that you can invest your money better than government can."

With that I'll let Steve have the last word here. The proposal in no way changes the number of shares of stock or which stocks the American public would hold for investment. So at the macro level, it is not the case of allowing the nation to "invest better than the government can." And Steve knows that, but it doesn't matter - he continues to peddle the same illogical story he knows is illogical. And he gets no criticism from the media apart from the misguided discussion as to whether stocks are a better investment than Social Security, will the bonds the government has to sell take away savings that could be used for investment, if the government risks its solvency by going even deeper into debt and all the other such nonsense we're calling innocent frauds.

Unfortunately, the deadly innocent frauds continuously compound and obscure any chance for legitimate analysis.

And it gets worse! The 'intergenerational' story continues something like this: "The problem is that 30 years from now there will be a lot more retired people and proportionately fewer workers (which is true), and the Social Security trust fund will run out of money (as if a number in a trust fund is an actual constraint on the government's ability to spend...silly, but they believe it). So to solve the problem, we need to figure out a way to be able to provide seniors with enough money to pay for the goods and services they will need." With this last statement it all goes bad. They assume that the real problem of fewer workers and more retirees, which is also known as the "dependency ratio," can be solved by making sure the retirees have sufficient funds to buy what they need.

Let's look at it this way: 50 years from now when there is one person left working and 300 million retired people (I exaggerate to make the point), that guy is going to be pretty busy since he'll have to grow all the food, build and maintain all the buildings, do the laundry, take care of all medical needs, produce the TV shows, etc. etc. etc. What we need to do is make sure that those 300 million retired people have the funds to pay him??? I don't think so! This problem obviously isn't about money.

What we need to do is make sure that the one guy working is smart enough and productive enough and has enough capital goods and software to be able to get it all done, or else those retirees are in serious trouble, no matter how much money they might have. So the real problem is, if the remaining workers aren't sufficiently productive, there will be a general shortage of goods and services. More "money to spend" will only drive up prices and not somehow create more goods and services. The mainstream story deteriorates further as it continues: "Therefore, government needs to cut spending or increase taxes today, to accumulate the funds for tomorrow's expenditures." By now I trust you know this is ridiculous and evident that the deadly innocent frauds are hard at work to undermine our well-being and the next generation's standard of living as well.

We know our government neither has nor doesn't have dollars. It spends by changing numbers up in our bank accounts and taxes by changing numbers down in our bank accounts. And raising taxes serves to lower our spending power, not to give the government anything to spend. It's OK if spending is too high, causing the economy to "overheat" (if we have too much spending power for what's for sale in that big department store called the economy). But if that's not the case, and in fact, spending is falling far short of what's needed to buy what's offered for sale at full employment levels of output, raising taxes and taking away our spending power only makes things that much worse.

And the story gets even worse. Any mainstream economist will agree that there pretty much isn't anything in the way of real goods we can produce today that will be useful 50 years from now. They go on to say that the only thing we can do for our descendants that far into the future is to do our best to make sure they have the knowledge and technology to help them meet their future demands. The irony is that in order

57

to somehow "save" public funds for the future, what we do is cut back on expenditures today, which does nothing but set our economy back and cause the growth of output and employment to decline. And worse yet, the great disappointment is that the first thing our misguided leaders cut back on is education - the one thing that the mainstream agrees *should* be done that actually helps our children 50 years down the road.

Should our policy makers ever actually get a handle on how the monetary system functions, they would realize that the issue is social equity, and possibly inflation, but never government solvency. They would realize that if they want seniors to have more income at any time, it's a simple matter of raising benefits, and that the real question is, what level of real resource consumption do we want to provide for our seniors? How much food do we want to allocate to them? How much housing? Clothing? Electricity? Gasoline? Medical services? These are the real issues, and yes, giving seniors more of those goods and services means less for us. The amount of goods and services we allocate to seniors is the real cost to us, not the actual payments, which are nothing more than numbers in bank accounts.

And if our leaders were concerned about the future, they would support the types of education they thought would be most valuable for that purpose. They don't understand the monetary system, though, and won't see it the "right way around" until they do understand it.

Meanwhile, the deadly innocent fraud of Social Security takes its toll on both our present and our future well-being.

### *Deadly Innocent Fraud #5:*

The trade deficit is an unsustainable imbalance that takes away jobs and output.

### *Facts:*

Imports are real benefits and exports are real costs. Trade deficits directly improve our standard of living. Jobs are lost because taxes are too high for a given level of government spending, not because of imports.

By now you might suspect that, once again, the mainstream has it all backwards, including the trade issue. To get on track with the trade issue, always remember this: In economics, it's better to receive than to give. Therefore, as taught in 1st year economics classes:

**Imports are real benefits. Exports are real costs.**

In other words, going to work to produce real goods and services to export for someone else to consume does you no economic good at all, unless you get to import and consume the real goods and services others produce in return. Put more succinctly: *The real wealth of a nation is all it produces and keeps for itself, plus all it imports, minus what it must export.*

A trade deficit, in fact, increases our real standard of living. How can it be any other way? So, the higher the trade deficit the better. The mainstream economists, politicians, and media all have the trade issue completely backwards. Sad but true.

To further make the point: If, for example, General MacArthur had proclaimed after World War II that since Japan had lost the war, they would be required to send the U.S. 2 million cars a year and get nothing in return, the result would have been a major international uproar about U.S. exploitation of conquered enemies. We would have been accused of fostering a repeat of the aftermath of World War I, wherein the allies demanded reparations from Germany which were presumably so high and exploitive that they caused World War II. Well, MacArthur did not order that, yet for over 60 years, Japan has, in fact, been sending us about 2 million cars per year, and we have been sending them little or nothing. And, surprisingly, they think that this means they are winning the "trade war," and we think it means that we are losing it. We have the cars, and they have the bank statement from the Fed showing which account their dollars are in.

Same with China - they think that they are winning because they keep our stores full of their products and get nothing in return, apart from that bank statement from the Fed. And our leaders agree and think we are losing. This is madness on a grand scale

Now take a fresh look at the headlines and commentary we see and hear daily:
- The U.S. is "suffering" from a trade deficit.
- The trade deficit is an unsustainable "imbalance."
- The U.S. is losing jobs to China.
- Like a drunken sailor, the U.S. is borrowing from abroad to fund its spending habits, leaving the bill to our children, as we deplete our national savings.

I've heard it all, and it's all total nonsense. We are benefiting IMMENSELY from the trade deficit. The rest of the world has been sending us hundreds of billions of dollars worth of real goods and services in excess of what we send to them. They get to produce and export, and we get to import and consume. Is this an unsustainable imbalance that we need to fix? Why would we want to end it? As long as they want to send us goods and services without demanding any goods and services in return, why should we not be able to take them?

There is no reason, apart from a complete misunderstanding of our monetary system by our leaders that has turned a massive real benefit into a nightmare of domestic unemployment.

Recall from the previous innocent frauds, the U.S. can ALWAYS support domestic output and sustain domestic full employment with fiscal policy (tax cuts and/or govt. spending), even when China, or any other nation, decides to send us real goods and services that displace our industries previously doing that work. All we have to do is keep American spending power high enough to be able to buy BOTH what foreigners want to sell us AND all the goods and services that we can produce ourselves at full employment levels. Yes, jobs may be lost in one or more industries. But with the right fiscal policy, there will always be sufficient domestic spending power to be able to employ those willing and able to work, producing other goods and services for our private and public consumption. In fact, up until recently, unemployment remained relatively low even as our trade deficit went ever higher.

So what about all the noise about the U.S. borrowing from abroad like a drunken sailor to fund our spending habits? Also not true! We are not dependent on China to buy our securities or in any way fund our spending. Here's what's really going on: Domestic credit creation is funding foreign savings.

What does this mean? Let's look at an example of a typical transaction. Assume you live in the U.S. and decide to buy a car made in China. You go to a U.S. bank, get accepted for a loan and spend the funds on the car. You exchanged the borrowed funds for the car, the Chinese car company has a deposit in the bank and the bank has a loan to you and a deposit belonging to the Chinese car company on their books. First, all parties are "happy." You would rather have the car than the funds, or you would not have bought it, so you are happy. The Chinese car company would rather have the funds than the car, or they would not have sold it, so they are happy. The bank wants loans and deposits, or it wouldn't have made the loan, so it's happy.

There is no "imbalance." Everyone is sitting fat and happy. They all got exactly what they wanted. The bank has a loan and a deposit, so they are happy and in balance. The Chinese car company has the $U.S. deposit they want as savings, so they are happy and in balance. And you have the car you want and a car payment you agreed to, so you are happy and in balance as well. Everyone is happy with what they have at that point in time.

And domestic credit creation - the bank loan - has funded the Chinese desire to hold a $U.S. deposit at the bank which we also call savings. Where's the "foreign capital?" There isn't any! The entire notion that the U.S. is somehow dependent on foreign capital is inapplicable. Instead, it's the foreigners who are dependent on our domestic credit creation process to fund their desire to save $U.S. financial assets. It's all a case of domestic credit funding foreign savings. We are not dependent on foreign savings for funding anything.

Again, it's our spreadsheet and if they want to save our dollars, they have to play in our sandbox. And what options do foreign savers have for their dollar deposits? They can do nothing, or they can buy other financial assets from willing sellers or they can buy real goods and services from willing sellers. And when they do that at market prices, again, both parties are happy. The buyers get what they want - real goods and services, other financial assets, etc. The sellers get what they want - the dollar deposit. No imbalances are possible. And there is not even the remotest possibility of U.S. dependency on foreign capital, as there is no foreign capital involved anywhere in this process.

### *Deadly Innocent Fraud #6:*

We need savings to provide the funds for investment.

### *Fact:*

Investment adds to savings.

Second to last but not the least, this innocent fraud undermines our entire economy, as it diverts real resources away from the real sectors to the financial sector, with results in real investment being directed in a manner totally divorced from public purpose. In fact, it's my guess that this deadly innocent fraud might be draining over 20% annually from useful output and employment - a staggering statistic, unmatched in human history. And it directly leads the type of financial crisis we've been going through.

It begins with what's called "the paradox of thrift" in the economics textbooks, which goes something like this: In our economy, spending must equal all income, including profits, for the output of the economy to get sold. (Think about that for a moment to make sure you've got it before moving on.) If anyone attempts to save by spending less than his income, at least one other person must make up for that by spending more than his own income, or else the output of the economy won't get sold.

Unsold output means excess inventories, and the low sales means production and employment cuts, and thus less total income. And that shortfall of income is equal to the amount not spent by the person trying to save. Think of it as the person who's trying to save (by not spending his income) losing his job, and then not getting any income, because his employer can't sell all the output.

So the paradox is, "decisions to save by not spending income result in less income and no new net savings." Likewise, decisions to spend more than one's income by going into debt cause incomes to rise and can drive real investment and savings. Consider this extreme example to make the point. Suppose everyone ordered a new pluggable hybrid car from our domestic auto industry. Because the industry can't currently produce that many cars, they would hire us, and borrow to pay us to first build the new factories to meet the new demand. That means we'd all be working on new plants and equipment - capital goods - and getting paid. But there would not yet be anything to buy, so we would necessarily be "saving" our money for the day the new cars roll off the new assembly lines. The decision to spend on new cars in this case results in less spending and more savings. And funds spent on the production of the capital goods, which constitute real investment, leads to an equal amount of savings.

I like to say it this way: ***Savings is the accounting record of investment.***

### Professor Basil Moore

I had this discussion with a Professor Basil Moore in 1996 at a conference in New Hampshire, and he asked if he could use that expression in a book he wanted to write. I'm pleased to report the book with that name has been published and I've heard it's a good read. (I'm waiting for my autographed copy.)

Unfortunately, Congress, the media and mainstream economists get this all wrong, and somehow conclude that we need more savings so that there will be funding for investment. What seems to make perfect sense at the micro level is again totally wrong at the macro level. Just as loans create deposits in the banking system, it is investment that creates savings.

So what do our leaders do in their infinite wisdom when investment falls, usually, because of low spending? They invariably decide "we need more savings so there will be more money for investment." (And I've never heard a single objection from any mainstream economist.) To accomplish this Congress uses the tax structure to create tax-advantaged savings incentives, such as pension funds, IRA's and all sorts of tax-advantaged institutions that accumulate reserves on a tax deferred basis. Predictably, all that these incentives do is remove aggregate demand (spending power). They function to keep us from spending our money to buy our output, which slows the economy and introduces the need for private sector credit expansion and public sector deficit spending just to get us back to even.

**This is why the seemingly-enormous deficits turn out not to be as inflationary as they might otherwise be.**

In fact it's the Congressionally-engineered tax incentives to reduce our spending (called "demand leakages") that cut deeply into our spending power, meaning that the government needs to run higher deficits to keep us at full employment. Ironically, it's the same Congressmen pushing the tax-advantaged savings programs, thinking we need more savings to have money for investment, that are categorically opposed to federal deficit spending.

And, of course, it gets even worse! The massive pools of funds (created by this deadly innocent fraud #6, that savings are needed for investment) also need to be managed for the further purpose of compounding the monetary savings for the beneficiaries of the future. The problem is that, in addition to requiring higher federal deficits, the trillions of dollars compounding in these funds are the support base of the dreaded financial sector. They employ thousands of pension fund managers whipping around vast sums of dollars, which are largely subject to government regulation. For the most part, that means investing in publicly-traded stocks, rated bonds and some diversification to other strategies such as hedge funds and passive commodity strategies. And, feeding on these "bloated whales," are the inevitable sharks - the thousands of financial professionals in the brokerage, banking and financial management industries who owe their existence to this 6th deadly innocent fraud.

### *Deadly Innocent Fraud #7:*
It's a bad thing that higher deficits today mean higher taxes tomorrow.

### *Fact:*
I agree - the innocent fraud is that it's a bad thing, when in fact it's a good thing!!!

Your reward for getting this far is that you already know the truth about this most common criticism of government deficits. I saved this for last so you would have all the tools to make a decisive and informed response.

First, why does government tax? Not to get money, but instead to take away our spending power if it thinks we have too much spending power and it's causing inflation.

Why are we running higher deficits today? Because the "department store" has a lot of unsold goods and services in it, unemployment is high and output is lower than capacity. The government is buying what it wants and we don't have enough after-tax spending power to buy what's left over. So we cut taxes and maybe increase government spending to increase spending power and help clear the shelves of unsold goods and services.

And why would we ever increase taxes? Not for the government to get money to spend - we know it doesn't work that way. We would increase taxes only when our spending power is too high, and unemployment has gotten very low, and the shelves have gone empty due to our excess spending power, and our available spending power is causing unwanted inflation.

So the statement "Higher deficits today mean higher taxes tomorrow" in fact is saying, "Higher deficits today, when unemployment is high, will cause unemployment to go down to the point we need to raise taxes to cool down a booming economy." Agreed!

# Part II: The Age of Discovery

I was born in the Manchester Memorial Hospital on September 18, 1949. My parents are Daniel and Muriel Mosler, and I was the oldest of three children. My brother Seth was born in 1951 and my sister Susan in 1955. We lived in an apartment on West Middle Turnpike before moving to a three-bedroom house at 47 Marion Drive in 1956. We lived there for about three years before selling the house and moving to a nearby rental due to financial difficulties. I attended Wadell School and then Buckley elementary school after we moved. I went to Illing Jr. High School and then Manchester High School where my father had also graduated in 1936.

We were what seemed to be a typical middle class Manchester family. My father worked as an accountant, tried managing a liquor store, sold life insurance and did tax preparation. My mother was an RN (registered nurse) and worked nights at Manchester Memorial Hospital.

I suspect I contracted my car disease at the age of maybe 8. I recall taking apart old lawn mowers and using the parts to make motorbikes and go-carts, using bolts and often wooden parts. Getting anything welded was a luxury outside of the family budget. And I might still be able to name on sight every U.S. car built from 1955 to 1975. I recall sitting on the sidewalk of the main road through town with my brother naming the cars as they drove by.

I had a variety of odd jobs in high school, including teaching kids to swim at a day camp, working at a local department store, mowing lawns and shoveling snow for the neighbors.

I got through high school with average grades, but my teachers always told me that I had "potential" if I would only apply myself. This was the standard assessment of the majority of American high school students, though I did do reasonably well on my SAT's, with a low 700 score in math and a low 600 score in the verbal section.

After I graduated from high school in 1967 (about 30TH out of a class of about 575), I attended the University of Connecticut, a public university, primarily because it only cost $300 per year for residents. Because I had accepted a $1,000 scholarship and a slide rule from a local organization to study engineering, I spent my first two years as an engineering student. I then switched my major to economics, and received a B.A. in 1971, which also happened to be the year things got bad enough for President Nixon to implement price and wage controls and take the United States off the gold standard internationally. We were in a recession, inflation had hit 3%, and France had tried to take their gold home from Fort Knox.

When I graduated in 1971, I experienced a recession first hand. I recall one job interview at National Cash Register that began with this friendly but resigned greeting from the hiring manager: *"I don't know why you and I are here. We're laying people off."*

I spent the next eighteen months working odd jobs, including a stint as a pool attendant in Miami Beach, where I put out mats and umbrellas for 25-cent tips and a $20 a week (GROSS) salary. To get by with paying me that little, the management also let me sleep in the storage room.

I finally got a real job in 1973, when I got a haircut and re-applied for a job at the Savings Bank of Manchester in my home town. (They told me after I was hired I was turned down the first time because my hair was too long.)

I started in the bank's personal loan department, where my first responsibility was to collect delinquent loans. Paul Coupe, the department head, handed me the collection books and added with a smile, "there's gold in them there books." Once a loan was delinquent, my job was to figure out how to get the money back. That could mean anything from phone calls to trying to get the borrower to make his payments to repossessing the car or other collateral and selling it for as much as possible. Collection methods also included home visits, using the legal system to secure legal judgments against the debtors and attaching bank accounts or garnishing wages to directly collect the money owed to the bank.

I quickly realized that this was where the rubber meets the road for the entire credit system. Without enforcement, there is no extension of credit. Loans were only as good as the ability to collect them. Years later, I would recognize this was also true of the currency itself, and that the value of the dollar was only as good as the federal government's ability to enforce tax collection.

After a year of doing collections, Paul gave me lending authority for loans up to $1,000. This was a responsibility I took very seriously. I was now responsible for lending other people's money, which for me was a far greater responsibility than lending my own money.

I remember having ongoing discussions with Paul on what could be called the "theory of lending" and the "logic of banking." The idea is that anyone can make loans so selectively that there will never be any losses. But the trick is to make loans where money might be lost, but where the odds were high enough so the interest the bank was making on the loans more than made up for the small amount of expected losses.

My collections experience brought home the nuances of what made loans go bad. It also made very clear that even with very high lending standards regarding the borrower's income, time on the job, home equity and past payment records, many other things could go wrong that could cause a borrower who looked like a very good risk at the outset to default. Job losses, illnesses, personal problems, car accidents and death all had some probability of taking place some percentage of the time. I understood that the lender would try and quantify all these risks before a loan was extended, and attempt to determine if the interest rate the bank intended to charge would be sufficient to cover the losses from loans that went bad, and still provide a good return to the bank.

Yes, we could tighten standards and reduce losses, but we would make very few loans and not be profitable. If we were too lax with our standards, we would make a lot more loans but the losses would eat up the profits. The answer was somewhere in between. The right answer to running a profitable bank, in the lending arena at least, lays somewhere in the middle of the two extremes of having standards that are too high and standards that are too low. As Paul used to tell me, when reviewing my loans that had gone bad, "If you aren't taking *some* losses, you're costing the bank money."

I currently own a "buy here pay here" used car lot. All of our borrowers are sub prime or less, and I make the lending decisions myself. Of every 100 new loans, 3 or 4 seem to go bad and cost me a few dollars after the car is repossessed and resold. And I still wonder with each application if I'm being too tight or too lax. After 40 years, the basic concepts of determining credit-worthiness still seem to hold.

Not long after I had been given lending authority, the bank foreclosed on a small (maybe 50 rooms) motel in downtown Manchester named Piano's, after the former owners. Paul sent me to manage it. The goal was to improve its operations sufficiently to get it sold as soon as possible, at as good a price as possible. We were in the banking business, and didn't want to be in the motel business.

When I arrived at the motel, I noticed that all the light bulbs were missing. "Welcome to what happens when borrowers go bad!" I thought to myself. The first thing I did was arrange to get some basic maintenance done to the motel, including some new light bulbs. I also began formulating a strategy to increase room revenues, so that a potential purchaser could see some actual cash flow, increasing the likelihood we could sell it.

First, I calculated the total monthly fixed expenses, assuming a 50% occupancy rate. Then, I did the math backwards, and calculated that if we could rent out half the rooms at $49 per week, we would break even. This was only $7 per day, a significantly lower rate than the going rate of $15 per day for most motels at the time. But once we had half the motel filled up at the relatively low weekly rate and all our expenses were covered, then the daily rents from the rest of the rooms would make us profitable. There seemed to be no risk to this strategy, but I needed to get approval from higher-ups at the bank.

I made a presentation to our bank's Vice President, Bill Johnson, where I outlined my strategy. Bill readily gave me the go-ahead. I put my first ad in the local paper announcing the new weekly rate, and within days the $49 per week rooms started filling up. I was pleasantly surprised and pleased that there was a demand for my new offering. As it turned out, quite a few respectable local professional people would occasionally have "domestic issues" and need a place to stay for a few weeks.

We got those rooms filled, and the motel started showing some profit. We soon sold it for a decent price and made a little profit on the original loan.

Not long after that, the president of the bank retired, and Bill Johnson took his job. Bill had been running the securities portfolio. I think Bill liked the way I had handled the motel foreclosure, so he promoted me to "investment officer" and I became the portfolio manager. While the portfolio was very small - only $5 million in stocks and $5 million in short-term investments - the scale of the responsibility seemed very large to me at the time. My previous lending authority had been only $5,000, and that had seemed large. Now I was responsible for $10 million of the bank's money.

My hands were shaking when I made my first call to purchase a $500,000 Certificate of Deposit for the bank. Don

Chardenierre of the Merrill Lynch office in Hartford was on the other end of the phone. I introduced myself to Don and asked for an interest rate offering from Merrill Lynch on the half a million dollars I wished to invest. Very politely, Don told me that the minimum investment they handled was $1 million, but that he would see what they could do for me. I thanked him and hung up the phone, now feeling very small!

Managing the bank's stocks meant attending meetings with our financial advisor, Ted Ladd of Standish, Ayers, and Woods in Boston. Bill, now our bank president and one of the finest human beings anyone can know, would take me to the meetings at the an old inn in Sturbridge, Mass., to meet with Ted and discuss our portfolio of equities, as well as external factors including the economy and the financial markets. We would also discuss possible changes in our holdings. Since Ted was given full discretion to manage the $5 million in our stock portfolio, there wasn't much for me to do in that half of the job.

But the other half of my job - managing our $5 million in short-term investments - was entirely managed in house, and I was free to come up with ideas to make the best of that money.

We had been keeping most of the $5 million in bank CDs (certificates of deposit) with maturities of about 6 months. At that time, we were paying 5.25% in interest to the depositors in our bank's savings accounts. This rate was fixed by law, and so all savings banks were paying that rate to their depositors. Unfortunately, we could only earn about 4% on our short-term investments in CDs, as that's where the Federal Reserve was setting short-term interest rates.

This seemed like an odd situation to me. During one of our regular management meetings at the bank, I suggested that instead of buying short-term CDs that paid us a 4% interest rate, we should simply go to another savings bank, and open a regular savings account that paid the 5.25% they were required by law to pay.

"We just put our money in a regular savings account at another savings bank at the 5.25% rate and let them worry about it!" I said in the meeting.

"Why would we help another bank by doing that?" asked one of the more senior executives.

My mentor and bank president Bill Johnson responded, "What will they do with the money, except take a loss?"

The skeptical executive had no answer to Bill's question, and his silence caused more than a little amusement at the meeting. The idea was approved.

The next day, I got in the car and started visiting other banks, trying to open a savings account for our bank. Several banks wouldn't accept our money. I remember a couple branch managers who were nearly in tears when their bosses turned down their request to accept our money for deposit into their bank.

"First they tell me to get deposits, and then you come in with $100,000, and they won't take it. What do they want me to do?" one of the branch managers moaned.

After a few days I finally managed to get my banks extra few hundred thousand dollars invested in savings accounts at other savings banks at the 5.25% rate--1.25% higher than what we would have received from CDs. (I asked for the free toasters the other banks were giving away at the time to anyone opening a new deposit, but not one of the banks would give me one!)

By now, after my experiences with the motel turnaround, and the improvement in the bank's return on short-term investments, I had a clear sense that I had an aptitude for the logic of finance. I had the ability to, now and then, see opportunities that others had overlooked.

About this time, there was a new type of mortgage-backed security, called a GNMA (pronounced "Ginny May") pass through. You could buy a GNMA pass through, and it would pay interest just like a mortgage investment. But you weren't getting a mortgage payment from a single property; you were buying a participation in a large pool of individual mortgages and getting your share of all the payments. And all the payments were fully guaranteed by the U.S. government, so there was no default risk. But, since the interest rates paid were a lot lower than the mortgage rates we were getting locally, it didn't make sense for our bank to invest in them.

However, I discovered something else was happening with GNMA securities. The Wall Street dealers were offering them for sale for future delivery dates. In other words, you could buy and sell them for delivery in the future. For instance, in March you could buy GNMA securities for delivery in March, but you could also buy them for delivery in June or even September. The price for these securities would be determined in March, but you didn't receive them or pay for them until the agreed-upon future delivery date. Also, the market prices to purchase the same GNMA security for delivery in March, June, or September differed. Something about this new kind of security and the price differential based upon the different time of delivery intrigued me. I started looking at the prices for the different delivery dates, trying to understand what they were based on. I somehow noticed that the prices were such that if I bought the GNMA's for March delivery, and at the same time sold them for June delivery, my actual earnings for that three month period would be higher than if I bought a 3-month CD for the bank, or put the funds in a savings account at another bank. Additionally, I discovered I could borrow the money to pay for the GNMA securities for the same 3 months at an even lower rate.

So I went back to our management team with a proposal. We could buy $1 million in GNMA's for March delivery, and at the same time sell them for June delivery, and the prices were such that we would earn a 5.5% annual rate on our money for that 90 day period. And, at the same time, our bank could borrow $1 million at only 4.5% for the same 90 days by using that same $1 million in GNMA's to secure our borrowing. This meant a locked-in profit for the bank - we borrowed at 4.5% and made 5.5% on the transaction. The management team approved the trades, and I booked my first fixed income mortgage-backed securities arbitrage profit. That's what the term "arbitrage" means - the simultaneous purchase and sale of the same securities, commodities or foreign exchange in different markets to profit from unequal prices."

That Friday night, at about 8 pm, I got a call at home from Jim Saxon from Salomon Brothers in New York City. He inquired, "Hi, I'm in a late sales meeting, and we are discussing your GNMA trade. Can you tell me one more time how it works?"

At the time, Salomon Brothers was the top Wall Street Fixed Income House. (Years later in the 1990's, they ran into a small market manipulation issue with U.S. Treasury and, as a result, were taken over by Citibank.) I found out later from three of their senior managers that during their high flying years in the 1980's, it was my ideas that had been instrumental in getting them named managing directors. These three managing directors went on to form a hedge fund, called Long Term Capital, where they developed their own ideas, this time with Nobel Prize winning economists.

In those early 1970's when I worked there, the Savings Bank of Manchester was one of those thousands of dull, boring savings banks that paid 5.25% to their depositors and financed homes with 8%, 30-year mortgages. We got to work at 8:30 am, and left to play golf (Or softball. My shoulder still isn't quite right from trying to throw someone out at the plate from the outfield) around 4 pm. And in 1972, with a U.S. population of just over 200 million, these plain, dumb, boring savings banks financed 2.6 million new housing starts, with no secondary markets, no futures markets, and very modestly paid employees (I started at $140 per week, and had worked my way up to $200 per week as an investment officer).

Today, with a population of over 300 million, a massive financial sector, untold financial innovations, and unlimited financial resources and liquidity, if we manage to get 2 million housing starts a year, it's proclaimed an unsustainable bubble. More on that kind of "progress" later in this book.

## Wall Street

George Weisse was a broker at Bache and Company, and he was one of the brokers on my list to call when we needed to do any transactions. We never did much actual business, but we did have several discussions of financial markets and trading strategies. George was doing very well with his brokerage business that focused on buying and selling public utility stocks.

In 1975, George was looking for an assistant who could both help him with his utility stock business and at the same time cover what were called second tier institutions for Bache's other products, including bonds and other fixed income securities. He offered me a starting salary of $15,000 a year, which was roughly 50% more than the bank was paying, and a chance to make more if successful. That year, I joined Bache as George's assistant. I remember getting into work one day with George talking on the phone while lying on the floor. I asked what happened. He said his back went out again. So I asked how it happened. He told me that he had been carrying big rocks up to his house from the river behind it. Turns out he had a bad back and this would happen on a regular basis. When it wasn't carrying rocks it was playing tennis or something like that. I got my SEC Series 7 license soon after I joined the firm, which qualified me to sell securities for life.

George was making serious money with his institutional equity sales, and was very, very good at what he did. He left Bache about a year after I got there, cutting himself a much better deal with Shearson. I stayed at Bache in Hartford, where I was now getting full commissions on all the clients for any business I could do. In my first month I made $5,000 which was a very high number for me. It was 1976. Life was good. And then I got another job offer.

Jay Pomerenze offered me a job on Wall Street with Bankers Trust Co. as an Assistant Vice President of Sales and Trading of GNMA securities. Jay was the GNMA trader at Bankers. I knew him from my Savings Bank of Manchester days. My primary contact at Bankers was Bill Lovern, who introduced me to Jay when I had become interested in GNMA's. Most memorable on my first trip to Wall St. was lunch at *Kabuki* where Bill took me for a new thing called sushi. Bill left Bankers for Weeden while I was still at Bache, and I had stayed in touch with Jay.

Jay said the job paid $30,000 a year. I said I was making $60,000 where I was ($5,000 the first month times 12 = $60,000). He said he'd go and talk to the higher-ups and got back to me with a $45,000 offer. I accepted.

I moved from Hartford, Conn. where I had been paying $125 a month for rent to New York City, where my one bedroom at 80th and York on the 20th floor was $525 a month. Federal taxes were 50%, and in New York City, state and local taxes took away about another 20%. I was taking home only about $350 a week from my gross pay of maybe $900. After rent, I was about back to where I was at the savings bank.

At Bankers, Jay and I pioneered the use of a variety of the new derivative products. These financial products were being introduced on the Chicago and New York futures markets at the time. They included new futures market contracts, various kinds of options and regular securities traded for future delivery dates.

I also recall discussions from those days that trace the history of my understanding of monetary operations. At some point while I was at Bankers, the Fed raised the discount rate. Our trading manager, Alan Rogers, said he hoped the Fed didn't just give the banks the money. He said the money supply was too high and the Fed needed to take some of it away. I thought about that for a moment and told him the Fed had to supply the money, as it couldn't come from anywhere else. The banking system was just a T account with assets and liabilities, and you can't just take away the assets. There is no such thing. He then said, "Well, there's $300 billion sloshing around in Europe, and they could use some of that." I replied that those were all T accounts as well and it wasn't a possibility, as a matter of accounting. The point here is I must have been thinking about that quite a bit back then, maybe in discussions with Jay and others, to have been able to use it with confidence in a relatively high-level discussion with the trading manager on the trading desk.

Well, Erich Heiniman, senior economist at Morgan Stanley, came out with the same position as Alan, which was published in the Wall St. Journal. My future partner, Cliff Viner, a portfolio manager at Phoenix Mutual Insurance in Hartford, directed me to the Morgan Stanley editorial that argued, as Alan did, that the Fed should not give the banks the funds this time. I told Cliff how it worked and why the Fed would necessarily "give" the banks the funds. Cliff called Morgan Stanley who gave him a double talk answer. I gave Cliff a response to that answer and he called them back. They then told Cliff that they retracted their position. The Fed, of course, added the reserves the next day with open market operations. The alternative would have been bank overdrafts, which carry a higher interest rate than the Fed's fed funds target, but are loans from the Fed nonetheless, though booked somewhat differently.

There are other examples as well. I recall Alan wondering where the $2 billion to buy the Treasury 2-year notes would come from. I answered it's the same money that they deficit spend that buys the Treasury notes. I don't know how or why

I came to know that type of thing back then, when no one else seemed to get it, including members of the Fed and Treasury.

In 1978, one of my clients, Colonial Mortgage, defaulted on an obligation to buy GNMA securities which I had sold to them. When the time had come to pay for the securities and take deliveries, they didn't have the money, and the price of the securities had gone down. So our trading desk sold them at a loss. This default occurred shortly after the credit department of Bankers Trust had sent a senior credit team to visit Colonial Mortgage, and after extensive analysis, had established their credit lines.

As an Assistant Vice President of Sales and Trading, my responsibilities were not to determine the credit-worthiness of my clients. In fact, I wasn't allowed to do that. That was the job of the credit department. My job was to help Bankers Trust make money by utilizing the credit lines that had been, after long analysis, established for that purpose.

Even though I had nothing to do with determining the credit-worthiness of Colonial Mortgage, I was assigned blame for their default. This was a first-hand view of corporate bureaucracy in action, as the various managers, including those on the credit team who had failed to accurately assess Colonial's credit worthiness, scrambled to avoid any responsibility. No one came to my defense. Enough said about this up-close look at institutional structure at work.

All along I was contributing quite a bit to the overall profits of the trading desk. One February, Jay was on vacation and I sat in to do the trading. February was a 28-day month that year, and month end was on a weekend.

Interest rates were something like 12%, and I knew GNMA securities paid interest based on a 30-day month even when there were only 28 days in the month. So I started making very tight markets for the sales force. In fact, I would offer to buy or sell GNMA's at the same price, with no spread at all. However, my bid (the price I would buy at) was for the Friday before month end, and my offered price was for the Monday following month end. The extra 2 days interest I would get for buying on Friday and selling for Monday at the same price was over $500 per million dollars worth of securities.

Because of the knowledge of the 2 days' free interest, our sales force had the highest bids and lowest offers of anyone on Wall St. - we did a lot of business, and made a lot of money. When the February trading results were announced in March, Alan Rodgers calmly read the results for each trader. For perspective, back then, making over $1 million a year in total profits for the entire trading floor was considered to be very good. Alan announced each trader individually: "2-year note trader - up $10,000, ten-year note trader - down $5,000...." And then he said: "GNMA - up $432,000, but that's just "carry." Turns out he was dismissive of the money I had made (not to mention the market share gained) because it wasn't made taking "real market risk."

When bonus time came around, things took another turn for the worse for me. My sales manager, Rich Molere, told me I wasn't getting a bonus because my business was mainly GNMA securities, and Bankers Trust was a "Government Bond Shop." I suggested he take a look at the accounts I was assigned and maybe help me get some government bond business from them. He looked through the list and realized that all of the accounts were mortgage bankers and savings & loan banks that did only GNMA business and none would ever do any bond business. So he said he'd give me some "bond accounts" to see what I could do.

The first was Chase Advisors, run by Bill Burke, who became a good friend of mine. The first thing I did was set up a "research meeting" where I visited them with Alan Lerner, our chief economist. We made a presentation to their group. That went well, and the next day, Chase "rewarded" us with an order for a few 2-year Treasury notes that made us about a $200 profit, if that. Rich congratulated me and said that that was more like it, that that was what he wanted to see.

The other account was Larry Burke at Oppenheimer. He was an aggressive government bond trader, and we started doing quite a bit of bond business (not all that profitable but certainly very active). The problem was that our trading desk wasn't quite ready for dealing with a "real" trader, so we missed a lot of business another firm would have done.

More interesting was the day Larry called me and said he had to get out of about $10 million long bonds right away. I knew our long bond trader, Paul Lagrande, wasn't in a position to make a competitive bid for that large a position. I suggested to Larry that he let Paul do the best he could in the broker's market and just take a small commission for helping him get the bonds sold. Larry agreed, and I told Paul he had an order to sell Larry's bonds the best he could, and take a $1500 markup, regardless of what price he got.

Well, Paul didn't get it. He had never been given an order to sell bonds like that. He got defensive and said, "There's a 99 ½ bid on the screen, but I can't pay that." I said I knew that and that I wasn't asking him to buy the bonds from Larry in advance. I explained that he just had to sell $10 million bonds to the brokers at the best price he could get. After a couple of back and forths, he sold the bonds to the brokers markets at a good price, then said "Now what do I do? I'm short!" I said, "You buy the bonds from Larry at the prices you sold them less the $1500, which is your profit." He wrote the tickets and was all smiles...and so was Larry. It was a win/win situation. I had proven to Rich that I could sell government bonds for Bankers Trust. I also knew that that and $10 would get me a cup of coffee.

Fortunately, another opportunity was developing for me. Buzz Newton, head of the Corporate Bond Department at William Blair and Company in Chicago, asked me to start a fixed income arbitrage department as part of his corporate bond department. Buzz was one of my clients at Bankers

Trust, and though he rarely did a trade with me, he liked my ideas and saw the value of bringing me in to implement those ideas.

I told Buzz I had a pretty good job at Bankers Trust. He explained that the position at Wm Blair and Co. had no salary. Instead, I would get a retail payout of 30% of my net profits. A very short time later I was in Chicago working at Blair.

## Chicago

Moving to Chicago from New York City was like taking off tight shoes. You don't realize they're tight until after you take them off. NYC might have 5 dry cleaners on every block and Chicago only one, but you only need one. It was the same with the people. Chicago allows people to be nicer, friendlier, with little or no edge. In NYC there's often aggression for no further purpose. It seemed an argumentative way of life compared to Chicago.

While I was at Wm Blair, I took on two partners: Justin Adams from the NYC office of First Boston, Corp. and Cliff Viner from Phoenix Mutual in Hartford, Connecticut. Justin was a GNMA trader at First Boston, working with Larry Fink, who went on to start Blackrock, which is probably the most successful asset management firm in the world. I got to know Justin while I was working at Bankers Trust. I filled in for Jay trading GNMA's when he was away on vacation. I remember at one point during the month of February, GNMA 8¼% securities trading for March delivery were ¾ of a point more expensive than they were for April delivery. It was very tempting to sell them short for March and at the same time buy them for April delivery, hoping that the spread would narrow before it was time to deliver the bonds I had sold for March delivery. The problem was that there were only a few weeks left for prices to "normalize" and there was the risk the spread would widen further and I'd be forced to close out my positions at a loss. While looking at the spread, it dawned on me to calculate how much I'd lose if I put the trade on and, worst case, simply failed to deliver the bonds I had sold short for March and didn't cover that fail until I took delivery of bonds I had bought for April delivery. It turned out that the loss would be only 5/8ths of a point. So selling March and buying April at a ¾ spread, with a 'worst case' of losing only 5/8 points if I failed to deliver the entire month of March, would still be a 1/8 point profit. And there was a fair chance that the spread would narrow some time before that and the actual profit would be larger. So I took this idea to Alan Rogers, the trading manager, and he rejected the idea, saying "Bankers Trust is not going to put on a position knowing it's going to fail to deliver on time." I tried to point out I didn't know we would fail, and in fact, I was hoping the spreads would narrow before that because the profit would be several times larger. Additionally, failing to deliver was not only "not a crime," the counterparty taking delivery actually preferred that you failed to deliver, as he then didn't have to pay for the bonds until you did deliver, and earned very high rates of interest on his money while waiting for you to deliver. In fact, Jay and I had made hundreds of thousands of dollars due to people failing to deliver to us. Alan would hear none of it. I then called Justin at First Boston and explained the trade, and why I wasn't allowed to do it. He immediately put several hundred million of it on for First Boston and had a very good month, providing liquidity for real investors and narrower spreads for them as well.

I knew Cliff from my time at Bache working for George Weiss. Cliff worked upstairs in the same building, managing 5 equity portfolios for Phoenix Mutual in Hartford. George knew Cliff and had me cover him for bonds. The first idea I showed Cliff was a UTC convertible bond that was selling only 1/32 above its actual conversion value. Cliff gave me an order to buy them at a price equal to the conversion value, which never did happen.

At Wm Blair, we were a very effective team. Justin and I worked on the trading strategies, while Cliff covered the handful of accounts that paid us commissions to piggyback onto our ideas. For the next five years, we were responsible for maybe 80% of Wm Blair's profits, which increased every year we were there, and we made lots of money for our clients as well.

A lot of those early profits came from arbitraging the newly-introduced futures contracts - the cash markets. We were among the first to grasp the concept of imbedded options in the various futures contracts. To give you an example of what all that means, when the new 10-year Treasury note futures contract was announced in the early 80's, the first thing we did was attempt to figure out what the correct prices for the futures contracts should be. The futures contract was a set of rules that told you what prices you would pay if you bought a futures contract, kept it until it expired and then took delivery of any of the eligible 10-year Treasury securities. And, as they still do today, every three months the U.S. Treasury would auction off billions of brand new 10-year Treasury notes. Knowing the current price of the eligible 10-year U.S. Treasury securities, one could calculate what the prices should be for the new 10-year Treasury futures contracts.

But there was another element. The new futures contracts would be for March, June, September, and December delivery dates, like all the other futures contracts. The first contract was for March delivery and the second for June delivery. However, what was different for March and June delivery was that the new 10-year note that would be auctioned in May would obviously not be deliverable in March, before it was issued, but would be eligible to be delivered in June. Additionally, at that time, each new 10-year note that the U.S. Treasury auctioned came at a higher yield than the older Treasury securities. This meant that the June contract should be expected to trade at a lower price than the March contract, because the new "cheaper" Treasury note to be auctioned in May would affect the June futures contract but not the March futures contract.

A week or so before the contract opened, the CBT (Chicago Board of Trade) conducted "practice trading" for the floor brokers. I inquired as to what the futures prices were for March and June for the practice trading session. Turned out that the March contract was trading at 100, and the June at 100½. We calculated that with the March contract at 100, June was only worth 99½. Seems that the floor traders doing the practice trading didn't realize that the new 10-year notes which would be auctioned in June would lower the value of the June contract, but not the March contract, which reflected the value of the current 10-year note.

With the opening of the new contract in just a few days, we started discussing which broker to use. About that time, we got a call from a Vince Ciaglia, who worked at a firm called Stotler. We'd never done much business with Vince, until this call. Vince started asking me what I thought the March/June spread should be. He wasn't sure and started asking what we thought the new 10-year Treasury note that would be deliverable in June might do to the spread. I told him that we were looking at the same thing and asked if he wanted our business for this trade in return for talking exclusively to us. He agreed. The next discussion with Vince was about which floor broker to use (the floor broker was the person down at the exchange who did the actual buying and selling in what was called the "futures pit," back before electronic trading) so that when our order was entered, the floor broker wouldn't scare the other traders. Vince had the ideal broker named Les. Les was a broker who worked in both the bean pit and the bond pit, and the last time he was in the bond pit, he had put his order in backwards and then had to go back in and trade his way out of his mistake.

When the 10-year futures market started trading on May 3, 1982, the first quotes had June about 1/8% higher than March. Not as good as we'd hoped for, but still a very long way from being ½% under March, which was what we thought was fair value. So we sent Les into the pit to buy 5,000 March contracts and sell 5,000 June contracts at the spread of 1/8%. Each contract represented $100,000 worth of Treasury securities, so this was a $500,000 order. Back then, a position like that could be "safely" taken on with less than $5 million in available capital.

Les went into the pit and came out a few minutes later, reporting all 5,000 done at our price. Seems the other brokers thought he was making another mistake, that he was supposed to be selling March and buying June based on where they thought prices should be from practice trading. So thinking there was easy money again coming their way, they filled his order out of their own trading accounts and then waited for him to discover his error and come back into the pit to try and reverse what he'd done and take another loss. Ten minutes later, when Les still hadn't come back, they suspected the worst - that he wasn't coming back, and they started scrambling to cover their positions as best as they could. I don't know what happened after that, except that over the next few weeks we made almost $3 million (back when that was a lot of money) as the March/June spread did indeed gravitate to what we had calculated as "fair value." It was a very good month for Wm Blair and Company.

On a look back, those five years I spent at William Blair in Chicago were my formative years. (Ned Janotta, the Senior Partner at Blair, remains one of the most astute, honorable and personable individuals one could possibly encounter, fortunately for me, as this next episode illustrates.) What could have been an unceremonious end instead turned out to be the beginning of the best of times for both Wm Blair and Company and for me as well.

It was early 1980. We had purchased 30-year U.S. Treasury bonds and sold the June delivery, 30-year bond futures contracts, which had become very expensive relative to the prices we were paying for the deliverable bonds. (The CBT had initiated a 30-year bond contract several years before it introduced the 10-year note futures in 1982) The prices of the bonds and the bond futures were such that if we held the bonds until June and then delivered them we would make a reasonably large profit. We knew of no reason why the spreads were so wide. It was like buying eggs from a farmer and selling them to the store and making a large profit. However, shortly after we put this trade on our books, the market changed dramatically, for unknown reasons, and it was suddenly possible to put the same trade in at prices that represented an even larger profit. While this is good news if you have more "dry powder" to add to your position, at the same time the position we already had in place was showing a substantial, $1 million loss. Let me give you an analogy to try to explain how this works. Suppose you are offered a free, $10 bill if you agree to come and pick it up in 30 days, and you take it. Then the next day things change and they are offering free $20 bill in 30 days. Sounds good, but now your first contract, to pick up the $10 bill in 30 days actually represents a loss of $10, because why would anyone take your $10 bill when there are currently $20 bills being offered? And so if you wanted to get out of your obligation to get a free $10 in 30 days, you would have to pay someone $10, so he could get the same $20 the other guy is offering. And, the real problem is that if you decide to stay with your contract to get a free $10 bill in 30 days, you have to now post $10 with the exchange so that if you take a hike and they have to liquidate your contract they don't have to take the $10 loss.

I immediately sat down with Ned, explaining that the position was to make us a $1 million profit when we delivered our bonds in June, but that the prices had changed, and we had to either meet a $1 million margin call, or close out the position and sustain a $1 million loss. He asked what would happen if we waited until June. I explained that we would get both our originally contracted $1 million profit and $1 million

89

in margin money back. I also said there was no guarantee the position wouldn't move further against us, but in any case by the June delivery date we'd get it all back plus $1 million.

Ned made the call, said he agreed with our plan to stay with the trade, and the meeting was over. Other Wall Street trading desks were not as fortunate. There were stories of their managers forcing them to exit their positions immediately at substantial losses.

Not long after that meeting, the prices of gold and silver collapsed, as did the Treasury note futures we had sold short, our margin money was returned and our expected profits were realized. And we also discovered what was happening behind the scenes. The billionaire Hunt brothers (back when that was a lot of money) had been buying the same Treasury futures we had been selling short with the profits they were making buying silver and driving prices up to almost $60/oz (today silver is still under $20/oz). That is what had caused our temporary "mark to market" loss. And it was the collapse of the gold and silver prices that forced the Hunt brothers to liquidate both their silver positions and their bond futures positions, and return our trade to profitability. What made this all the more interesting was how that happened. It seems the owners of the COMEX, the NY exchange where the silver futures were traded, sold short for their personal accounts when silver went over $50/oz, and then drastically raised margin requirements for the Hunts, forcing them to liquidate and lose billions (and restoring our profits) as the price of silver dropped to under $10/oz. And this was all perfectly legal at the time.

In 1982, Justin, Cliff and I were aware the markets were large enough for us to manage more capital without hurting our returns for our investors. It didn't make sense to do that within the legal structure of a broker-dealer like William Blair. Ned helped us to raise more capital and keep the business separate from William Blair. We formed our own company, Illinois Income Investors, (later shortened to III), with Wm

Blair and Company as one of our partners.

Illinois Income Investors specialized in fixed income arbitrage, utilizing both actual securities and related derivative products, with a market neutral/0 duration strategy. That meant we promised no interest rate exposure, rates going up or down were not supposed to be a factor in the level of profits. We were paid 35% of the profits but no fixed management fees.

Over the next fifteen years, we continued the success we'd had at William Blair and Company. Including the time at Blair, we established a 20-year track record (from 1978 to 1997) with only one losing month, a drop of a tenth of one percent on a mark to market that reversed the next month, and no losing trades that any of us can recall. III was ranked Number One in the world for the highest risk-adjusted spreads by *Managed Account Reports* through 1997. When I stepped down, Cliff Viner took control of about $3.5 billion in capital and $35 billion in assets. The 1996 drama with the Tokyo Futures exchange along with philosophical differences with a new partner told me it was a good time to take a break.

The designation for the September 1996 futures contract for the 10-year JGB's (Japanese government bonds) was JBU6, which at one time was to be the title of this book, before the term "innocent fraud" was coined. This time, again for some unknown reason, the JBU6 (the September futures contract) was, to me, mispriced. But this time it was on the Tokyo exchange, this time it was too cheap, this time there was a large interest rate swap market and this time we had over $3 billion under management, bwtwalom (back when that was a lot of money). Slowly, over the months leading up to September, we and our clients began to buy the JBU6 and pay fixed on 7 to 10-year yen labor swaps. Without going into a lot more detail, it's enough to understand that paying a fixed rate on a swap was roughly equivalent to selling real bonds short. So we were using the cheap futures market to buy bonds and sell them at what we thought was a higher price via the interest rate swap market. The position got very large, approaching 7,500 contracts, which represented over $7 billion worth of bonds (yes, bwtwalom). Around then, we noticed that we had contracted to take delivery of more of the cheapest to deliver JGB's than the government of Japan had issued. That added a new dimension. If we took delivery, the other side would have to give us something, and if the cheapest bonds to deliver weren't available, they would be forced to deliver more expensive bonds to us, which meant higher profits. And, if supply of that more expensive bond was exhausted, they would be forced to deliver an even more expensive bond.

While this looked very attractive to us, the nagging question was why anyone would be selling us the futures contracts at what looked to be very low prices. Additionally, at this point, the September futures contract also looked cheap vs. the December '06 and March '07 futures prices, so we also bought September and sold December and March futures. But the futures remained cheap and we kept adding to our position. We got up to over 14,000 contracts for III and for our AVM clients before the delivery date, and the futures were still cheap. Astounding! I had our repo trader check to see if the bonds we were expecting to be delivered were available to be borrowed. I was guessing the dealers who had sold short to us were maybe going to deliver borrowed bonds to us. But no, there were still bonds to be borrowed - and borrowed relatively cheaply. So we borrowed the bonds ourselves to make sure that no one did an end run around us, and tried to deliver borrowed bonds, not that it mattered all that much if they did, but I wasn't keen on taking any chances at this point.

The next step was finding a dealer who we could use to take delivery. I was hoping to find one who had the same trade on so we could take delivery on the combined positions. I found Craig Foster at Credit Suisse in Tokyo. He was long about 7,000 contracts and had a similar trade on. Perfect! One last piece, if we were to take delivery of what was now some $20 billion of JGB's (still a lot of money), we needed to borrow the money to pay for them. Craig made the call to Switzerland and relayed the good news; he had a $20 billion line from his home office. We were bullet proof.

When the notice day came, the day when the other side has to tell you what bonds they are delivering to you, we were notified that the other side was mostly going to deliver to us the cheapest bonds possible. Fine, except that there weren't that many. We considered the possibility that they somehow had gotten extra bonds that didn't previously exist from the Bank of Japan. Then we started getting the calls asking us to lend them the bonds they needed to deliver to us and wanted to know what price we would charge them. This was madness! They had to have the bonds. They were committed to deliver them to us, and the penalty for failing to deliver was absolute dismissal from the yen bond markets and unknown fines from the Bank of Japan for disrupting their financial system. We were on the good side, buying Japans bonds via their futures market. They like people to buy their bonds. It was the other side that had the explaining to do. They had been selling billions of Japan's bonds short and didn't even have any to deliver. The Bank of Japan did some serious wrist slapping over that.

Well, we did lend them the bonds, but at a price. Since we did need the dealers to stay in business, we let them out at a price of about half of what they probably would have charged us had the situation been reversed (maybe a lot less than half). Perhaps we should have been tougher on them, but we walked away with about $150 million in profits for our side and went on record as having engineered the largest futures delivery of all time, last I checked.

### Italian Epiphany

I now backtrack to the early 1990's, to conclude this narrative leading up to the seven deadly innocent frauds. It was then that circumstances led me to the next level of understanding of the actual functioning of a currency.

Back then, it was the government of Italy, rather than the United States, which was in crisis. Professor Rudi Dornbusch, an influential academic economist at MIT, insisted that Italy was on the verge of default because their debt-to-GDP ratio exceeded 110% and the lira interest rate was higher than the Italian growth rate.

Things were so bad that Italian Government Securities denominated in lira yielded about 2% more than the cost of borrowing the lira from the banks. The perceived risk of owning Italian government bonds was so high that you could buy Italian government securities at about 14%, and borrow the lira to pay for them from the banks at only about 12% for the full term of the securities. This was a free lunch of 2%, raw meat for any bond desk like mine, apart from just one thing; the perceived risk of default by the Italian government. There was easy money to be made, but **only** if you knew for sure that the Italian government wouldn't default.

The "Free Lunch" possibility totally preoccupied me. The reward for turning this into a risk free spread was immense. So I started brainstorming the issue with my partners. We knew no nation had ever defaulted on its own currency when it was not legally convertible into gold or anything else.

There was a time when nations issued securities that were convertible into gold. That era, however, ended for good in 1971 when President Nixon took us off the gold standard internationally (the same year I got my BA from U-Conn) and we entered the era of floating exchange rates and non convertible currencies.

While some people still think that the America dollar is backed by the gold in Fort Knox, that is not the case. If you take a $10 bill to the Treasury Department and demand gold for it, they won't give it to you because they simply are not legally allowed to do so, even if they wanted to. They will give you two $5 bills or ten $1 bills, but forget about getting any gold.

Historically, government defaults came only with the likes of gold standards, fixed exchange rates, external currency debt, and indexed domestic debt. But why was that? The answer generally given was "because they can always print the money." Fair enough, but there were no defaults (lots of inflation but no defaults) and no one ever did "print the money," so I needed a better reason before committing millions of our investors funds.

A few days later when talking to our research analyst, Tom Shulke, it came to me. I said, "Tom, if we buy securities from the Fed or Treasury, functionally there is no difference. We send the funds to the same place (the Federal Reserve) and we own the same thing, a Treasury security, which is nothing more than account at the Fed that pays interest."

So functionally it has to all be the same. Yet presumably the Treasury sells securities to fund expenditures, while when the Fed sells securities, it's a "reserve drain" to "offset operating factors" and manage the fed funds rate. Yet they have to be functionally the same - it's all just a glorified reserve drain!

Many of my colleagues in the world of hedge fund management were intrigued by the profit potential that might exist in the 2% free lunch that the Government of Italy was offering us. Maurice Samuels, then a portfolio manager at Harvard Management, immediately got on board, and set up meetings for us in Rome with officials of the Italian government to discuss these issues.

Maurice and I were soon on a plane to Rome. Shortly after landing, we were meeting with Professor Luigi Spaventa, a senior official of the Italian Government's Treasury Department. (I recall telling Maurice to duck as we entered the room. He looked up and started to laugh. The opening was maybe twenty feet high. "That's so you could enter this room in Roman times carrying a spear," he replied.)

Professor Spaventa was sitting behind an elegant desk. He was wearing a three-piece suit, and smoking one of those curled pipes. The image of the great English economist John Maynard Keynes, whose work was at the center of much economic policy discussion for so many years, came to mind. Professor Spaventa was Italian, but he spoke English with a British accent, furthering the Keynesian imagery.

After we exchanged greetings, I opened with a question that got right to the core of the reason for our trip. "Professor Spaventa, this is a rhetorical question, but why is Italy issuing Treasury securities? Is it to get lira to spend, or is it to prevent the lira interbank rate falling to zero from your target rate of 12%?" I could tell that Professor Spaventa was at first puzzled by the questions. He was probably expecting us to question when we would get our withholding tax back. The Italian Treasury Department was way behind on making their payments. They had only two people assigned to the task of remitting the withheld funds to foreign holders of Italian bonds, and one of these two was a woman on maternity leave.

Professor Spaventa took a minute to collect his thoughts. When he answered my question, he revealed an understanding of monetary operations we had rarely seen from Treasury officials in any country. "No," he replied. "The interbank rate would only fall to ½%, NOT 0%, as we pay ½% interest on reserves." His insightful response was everything we had hoped for. Here was a Finance Minister who actually understood monetary operations and reserve accounting! (Note also that only recently has the U.S. Fed been allowed to pay interest on reserves as a tool for hitting their interest rate target)

I said nothing, giving him more time to consider the question. A few seconds later he jumped up out of his seat proclaiming "Yes! And the International Monetary Fund is making us act pro cyclical!" My question had led to the realization that the IMF was making the Italian Government tighten policy due to a default risk that did not exist.

Our meeting, originally planned to last for only twenty minutes, went on for two hours. The good Professor began inviting his associates in nearby offices to join us to hear the good news, and instantly the cappuccino was flowing like water. The dark cloud of default had been lifted. This was time for celebration!

A week later, an announcement came out of the Italian Ministry of Finance regarding all Italian government bonds - "No extraordinary measures will be taken. All payments will be made on time." We and our clients were later told we were the largest holders of Italian lira denominated bonds outside of Italy, and managed a pretty good few years with that position.

Italy did not default, nor was there ever any solvency risk. Insolvency is never an issue with nonconvertible currency and floating exchange rates. We knew that, and now the Italian Government also understood this and was unlikely to "do something stupid," such as proclaiming a default when there was no actual financial reason to do so. Over the next few years, our funds and happy clients made well over $100 million in profits on these transactions, and we may have saved the Italian Government as well. The awareness of how currencies function operationally inspired this book and hopefully will soon save the world from itself.

As I continued to consider the ramifications of government solvency not being an issue, the ongoing debate over the U.S. budget deficit was raging. It was the early 1990's, and the recession had driven the deficit up to 5% of GDP (deficits are traditionally thought of as a percent of GDP when comparing one nation with another, and one year to another, to adjust for the different sized economies).

Gloom and doom were everywhere. News anchor David Brinkley suggested that the nation needed to declare bankruptcy and get it over with. Ross Perot's popularity was on the rise with his fiscal responsibility theme. Perot actually became one of the most successful 3rd party candidates in history by promising to balance the budget. (His rising popularity was cut short only when he reportedly claimed the Viet Cong were stalking his daughter's wedding in Texas.)

With my new understanding, I was keenly aware of the risks to the welfare of our nation. I knew that the larger federal deficits were what was *fixing* the broken economy, but I watched helplessly as our mainstream leaders and the entire media clamored for fiscal responsibility (lower deficits) and were prolonging the agony.

It was then that I began conceiving the academic paper that would become *Soft Currency Economics*. I discussed it with my previous boss, Ned Janotta, at William Blair. He suggested I talk to Donald Rumsfeld (his college roommate, close friend and business associate), who personally knew many of the country's leading economists, about getting it published. Shortly after, I got together with "Rummy" for an hour during his only opening that week. We met in the steam room of the Chicago Racquet Club and discussed fiscal and monetary policy. He sent me to Art Laffer who took on the project and assigned Mark McNary to co-author, research and edit the manuscript, which was completed in 1993.

*Soft Currency Economics* remains at the head of the "mandatory readings" list at www.moslereconomics.com where I keep a running blog. It describes the workings of the monetary system, what's gone wrong and how gold standard rhetoric has been carried over to a nonconvertible currency with a floating exchange rate and is undermining national prosperity.

## **Part III:** Public Purpose

Functions of government are those that best serve the community by being done collectively. These include: The military, the legal system, international relations, police protection, public health (and disease control), public funding for education, strategic stockpiles, maintaining the payments system, and the prevention of "races to the bottom" between the states, including environmental standards, enforcement standards, regulatory standards and judicial standards.

What has made the American economy the envy of the world has been that people working for a living make sufficient take-home pay in order to be able to purchase the majority of the goods and services they desire and are produced. And what American business does is compete for those dollars with the goods and services they offer for sale. Those businesses that produce goods and services desired by consumers are often rewarded with high profits, while those that fail fall by the wayside. The responsibility of the federal government is to keep taxes low enough so that people have the dollars to spend to be able to purchase the goods and services they prefer from the businesses of their choice.

Today, unfortunately, we are being grossly overtaxed for the current level of government spending, as evidenced by the high level of unemployment and the high level of excess capacity in general. People working for a living are getting squeezed, as they are no longer taking home a large enough pay check to cover their mortgage payments, car payments and various routine expenses, nevermind any extra luxuries.

To address the current financial crisis and economic collapse, I recommend a number of proposals in the pages ahead.

## A Payroll Tax Holiday

I recommend that an immediate "payroll tax holiday" be declared whereby the U.S. Treasury makes all FICA (Social Security and Medicare) payroll tax deductions for all employees and employers. This proposal will increase the take-home pay of a couple making a combined $100,000 per year by over $650 per month, restoring their ability to make their mortgage payments, meet their routine expenses, and even do a little shopping. People with money to spend will immediately lead to a pickup in business sales, which will quickly result in millions of new jobs to serve the increased demand for goods and services. And people able to make their mortgage and loan payments is exactly what the banking system needs most to quickly return to health, not government funding that can only keeps them limping along with loans that continue to default. The only difference between a good loan and a bad loan is whether or not the borrower can make his payment.

## Revenue sharing

My second proposal is to give the U.S. state governments an immediate, unrestricted $150 billion of revenue sharing on a per capita basis (about $500 per capita). Most of the states are in dire straights as the recession has cut into their normal revenue sources. By pushing back federal funds on a per capita basis, it will be "fair" to all and not specifically "reward bad behavior." This distribution will give the states the immediate relief they need to sustain their essential services. As the economy recovers, their revenues will increase to pre-recession levels and beyond.

## National Service Jobs

The next recommendation of mine is to fund an $8/hour national service job for anyone willing and able to work; this will include child care, the current federal medical coverage and all of the other standard benefits of federal employees. This is a critical step to sustain growth and foster price stability. This provides a transition from unemployment to private sector employment. Businesses tend to resist hiring the unemployed, and especially the long-term unemployed. This national service job provides a transition from unemployment to employment, and, as the economy recovers (due to my first two proposals), businesses will hire from this pool of labor to meet their needs for more workers.

## Universal Health Care Coverage

My proposal regarding health care is to give everyone over the age of 18 a bank account that has, perhaps, $5,000 in it, to be used for medical purposes. $1,000 is for preventative measures and $4,000 for all other medical expenses. At the end of each year, any unspent funds remaining of the $4,000 portion are paid to that individual as a "cash rebate." Anything above $5,000 would be covered by a form of Medicare. There would be no restrictions on purchasing private insurance policies.

This proposal provides for universal health care, maximizes choice, employs competitive market forces to minimize costs, frees up physician time previously spent in discussion with insurance companies, rewards "good behavior" and reduces insurance company participation. This will greatly reduce demands on the medical system, substantially increasing the supply of available doctor/patient time and makes sure all Americans have health care. To ensure preventative measures are taken, the year-end rebate can be dependent, for example, on the individual getting an annual check up. And though it is federally funded, it can be administered by the states, which could also set standards and requirements.

There is no economic school of thought that would suggest health care should be what's called a "marginal cost of production" means that it is bad for the economy and our entire standard of living to have business pay for health care. This proposal eliminates that problem for the American economy in a way that provides health care for everyone, saves real costs, puts the right incentives in place, promotes choice and directs competitive forces to work in favor of public purpose.

### Proposals for the Monetary System

First, the Federal Reserve should immediately lend to its member banks on an unsecured basis, rather than demanding collateral for its loans. Demanding collateral is both redundant and obstructive. It is redundant because member banks can already raise government-insured deposits and issue government-insured securities in unlimited quantities without pledging specific collateral to secure those borrowings. In return, banks are subject to strict government regulation regarding what they can do with those insured funds they raise, and the government continuously examines and supervises all of its member banks for compliance. With the government already insuring bank deposits and making sure only solvent banks continue to function, the government is taking no additional risk by allowing the Federal Reserve to lend to its member banks on an unsecured basis. With the Federal Reserve lending unsecured to its member banks, liquidity would immediately be normalized and no longer be a factor contributing to the current financial crisis or any future financial crisis.

Second, the government should also remove the $250,000 cap on insured bank deposits, as well as remove regulations pertaining to bank liquidity, at the same time that it allows the Federal Reserve to lend unsecured to member banks. The Federal Reserve should lower the discount rate to the fed funds rate (and, as above, remove the current collateral requirements). The notion of a "penalty" rate is inapplicable with today's non-convertible currency and floating exchange rate policy.

Third, an interbank market serves no public purpose. It can be eliminated by having the Federal Reserve offer loans to member banks for up to 6 months, with the FOMC (Federal Open Market Committee, the collection of Fed officials who meet and vote on monetary policy) setting the term structure of rates at its regular meetings. This would also replace many of the various other lending facilities the FOMC has been experimenting with.

Fourth, have the Treasury directly fund the debt of the FHLB (Federal Home Loan Bank) and FNMA (the Federal National Mortgage Association), the U.S. Federal housing agencies. This will reduce their funding costs, and this savings will be directly passed on to qualifying home buyers. There is no reason to give investors today's excess funding costs currently paid by those federal housing agencies when the full faith and credit of the US government is backing them.

Fifth, have FNMA and the FHLB "originate and hold" any mortgages they make, and thereby eliminate that portion of the secondary mortgage market. With Treasury funding, secondary markets do not serve public purpose.

Sixth, increase and vigorously enforce mortgage fraud penalties with Federal agencies.

## Strategic Stockpiles

When families live on remote farms, for example, it makes sense to store perhaps a year or more of food for crop failures and other potential disruptions of the food supply. However, families living in cities, as a practical matter, instead can only save U.S. dollars. Unfortunately, in the event of actual shortages of food and other strategic supplies, numbers in bank accounts obviously will not do the trick. It is therefore a matter of public purpose to insure that there are actual strategic reserves for emergency consumption. Currently we have a strategic oil reserve. This should be extended to stores of other necessities for the purpose of emergency consumption. The purpose should not be to support special interest groups, but to provide the consumer with real supplies of actual consumables for rainy days.

## A Housing Proposal for the Financial Crisis:

1) If the owner of a house about to be foreclosed wants to remain in the house, he notifies the government, which then buys the house during the foreclosure sale period from the bank at the lower of fair market value or the remaining mortgage balance.

2) The government rents the house to the former owner at a fair market rent.

3) After two years, the house is offered for sale and the former owner/renter has the right of first refusal to buy it. While this requires a lot of direct government involvement and expense, and while there is room for dishonesty at many levels, it is far superior to any of the proposed plans regarding public purpose, which includes:

    a) Keeping people in their homes via affordable rents;

    b) Not interfering with existing contract law for mortgage contracts;

    c) Minimizing government disruption of outcomes
       for mortgage backed securities holders;
    d) Minimizing the moral hazard issue.

With this proposal, the foreclosure process is allowed to function according to law, so no contracts are violated. And renting to the former owner at a fair market rent is not a subsidy, nor is the repurchase option at market price a subsidy.

## How We Can All Benefit from the Trade Deficit

The current trade gap is a reflection of the rest of the world's desires to save U.S. financial assets. The only way the foreign sector can do this is to net export to the U.S. and keep U.S. dollars as some form of dollar financial assets (cash, securities, stocks, etc). So the trade deficit is not a matter of the U.S. being dependent on borrowing offshore, as pundits proclaim daily, but a case of offshore investors desiring to hold U.S. financial assets. To accomplish their savings desires, foreigners vigorously compete in U.S. markets by selling at the lowest possible prices. They go so far as to force down their own domestic wages and consumption in their drive for "competitiveness," all to our advantage. If they lose their desire to hold U.S. dollars, they will either spend them here or not sell us products to begin with, in which case that will mean a balanced trade position. While this process could mean an adjustment in the foreign currency markets, it does NOT cause a financial crisis for the U.S. The trade deficit is a boon to the US. There need not be a "jobs issue" associated with it. Appropriate fiscal policy can always result in Americans having enough spending power to purchase both our own full employment output and anything the foreign sector may wish to sell us. The right fiscal policy works to optimize our output, employment and standard of living, given any size trade gap.

## Industries with Strategic Purpose

Our steel industry is an example of a domestic industry with important national security considerations. Therefore, I would suggest that rather than continuing with the general steel tariffs recently implemented, defense contractors should be ordered to use only domestic steel. This will ensure a domestic steel industry capable of meeting our defense needs, with defense contractors paying a bit extra for domestically-produced steel, while at the same time lowering the price for non-strategic steel consumption for general use.

## Using a Labor Buffer Stock to let Markets Decide the Optimum Deficit

To optimize output, substantially reduce unemployment, promote price stability and use market forces to immediately promote health-care insurance nationally, the government can offer an $8 per hour job to anyone willing and able to work that includes full federal health-care benefits. To execute this program, the government can first inform its existing agencies that anyone hired at $8 per hour "doesn't count" for annual budget expenditures. Additionally, these agencies can advertise their need for $8 per hour employees with the local government unemployment office, where anyone willing and able to work can be dispatched to the available job openings. This job will include full benefits, including health care, vacation, etc. These positions will form a national labor "buffer stock" in the sense that it will be expected that these employees will be prone to being hired away by the private sector when the economy improves. As a buffer stock program, this is highly countercyclical anti-inflationary in a recovery, and anti-deflationary in a slowdown. Furthermore, it allows the market to determine the government deficit, which automatically sets it at a near "neutral" level. In addition to the direct benefits of more output from more workers, the indirect benefits of full employment should be very high as well. These include increased family coherence, reduced domestic violence, less crime, and reduced incarcerations. In particular, teen and minority employment should increase dramatically, hopefully, substantially reducing the current costly levels of unemployment.

## Interest Rates and Monetary Policy

It is the realm of the Federal Reserve to decide the nation's interest rates. I see every reason to keep the "risk free" interest rate at a minimum, and let the market decide the subsequent credit spreads as it assesses risk.

Since government securities function to support interest rates, and not to finance expenditure, they are not necessary for the operation of government. Therefore, I would instruct the Treasury to immediately cease issuing securities longer than 90 days. This will serve to lower long-term rates and support investment, including housing. Note, the Treasury issuing long term securities and the Fed subsequently buying them, as recently proposed, is functionally identical to the Treasury simply not issuing those securities in the first place.

I would also instruct the Federal Reserve to maintain a Japan like 0% fed funds rate. This is not inflationary nor is it the cause of currency depreciation, as Japan has demonstrated for over 10 years. Remember, for every $ borrowed in the banking system, there is a $ saved. Therefore, changing rates shifts income from one group to another. The net income effect is zero. Additionally, the non government sector is a net holder of government securities, which means there are that many more dollars saved than borrowed. Lower interest rates mean lower interest income for the non-government sector. Thus, it is only if the borrower's propensity to consume is substantially higher than that of savers does the effect of lower interest rates become expansionary in any undesirable way. And history has shown this never to be the case. Lower long term rates support investment, which encourages productivity and growth. High risk-free interest rates support those living off of interest payments (called rentiers), thereby reducing the size of the labor force and consequently reducing real national output.

## The Role of Government Securities

It is clear that government securities are not needed to "fund" expenditures, as all spending is but the process of crediting a private bank account at the Fed. Nor does the selling of government securities remove wealth, as someone buying them takes funds from his bank account (which is a U.S. financial asset) to pay for them, and receives a government security (which is also a U.S. financial asset). Your net wealth is the same whether you have $1 million in a bank account or a $1 million Treasury security. In fact, a Treasury security is functionally nothing more than a time deposit at the Fed.

Nearly 20 years ago, *Soft Currency Economics* was written to reveal that government securities function to support interest rates, and not to fund expenditures as generally perceived. It goes through the debits and credits of reserve accounting in detail, including an explanation of how government, when the Fed and Treasury are considered together, is best thought of as spending first, and then offering securities for sale. Government spending adds funds to member bank reserve accounts. If Govt. securities are not offered for sale, it's not that government checks would bounce, but that interest rates would remain at the interest rate paid on those reserve balances.

In the real world, we know this must be true. Look at how Turkey functioned for over a decade - quadrillions of liras of deficit spending, interest rate targets often at 100%, inflation nearly the same, continuous currency depreciation and no confidence whatsoever. Yet government "finance" in lira was never an issue. Government lira checks never bounced. If they had been relying on borrowing from the markets to sustain spending, as the mainstream presumed they did, they would have been shut down long ago. Same with Japan – over 200% total government debt to GDP, 7% annual deficits, downgraded below Botswana, and yet government yen checks never bounced, and 3-month government securities fund near 0%. Again, clearly, funding is not the imperative.

The U.S. is often labeled "the world's largest debtor." But what does it actually owe? For example, assume the U.S. government bought a foreign car for $50,000. The government has the car, and a non-resident has a U.S. dollar bank account with $50,000 in it, mirroring the $50,000 his bank has in its account at the Fed that it received for the sale of the car. The non-resident now decides that instead of the non-interest bearing demand deposit, he'd rather have a $50,000 Treasury security, which he buys from the government. Bottom line: the US government gets the car and the non-resident holds the government security. Now what exactly does the U.S. government owe? When the $50,000 security matures, all the government has promised is to replace the security held at the Fed with a $50,000 (plus interest) credit to a member bank reserve account at the Fed. One financial asset is exchanged for another. The Fed exchanges an interest bearing financial asset (the security) with a non-interest bearing asset. That is the ENTIRE obligation of the U.S. government regarding its securities. That's why debt outstanding in a government's currency of issue is never a solvency issue.

### Children as an Investment Rather than an Expense

Anyone who pauses to think about it will realize that our children are our fundamental real investment for the future. It should be obvious to all that without children, there won't be much human life left in 100 years. However, our current

109

institutional structure - the tax code and other laws and incentives on the books - have made our children an expense rather than an investment. And a lot of behavior most of us would like to see not happen, including deficiencies in education, child neglect and abuse and high rates of abortion, could be addressed by modifying the incentives built into our financial system.

## Public Purpose

For me, all federal public policy begins and ends with public purpose. I begin with a brief list of the functions of government, all of which comprise what can be called public infrastructure, that in my estimation do serve public purpose and should be provisioned accordingly.

The first is defense. It is my strong belief that without adequate military defenses, the world's democracies (a word I'll use for most forms of representative governments) are at risk of physical invasion and domination by nations with dictatorships and other related forms of totalitarianism. While democracies will move to defend themselves, in today's world, it is most often the dictatorships that move militarily to attack other nations without the provocation of a military threat. Examples include Pakistan threatening India, North Korea threatening not only South Korea but others in the region, Russia supporting military actions against most any western democracy, Israel under constant threat of attack by all the region's dictatorships and the Taliban attempting to take control of Afghanistan and disrupt any attempt at establishing representative government. It is evident to me that if the western democracies decided to abandon all defense measures they would immediately become subject to hostile invasion on multiple fronts. Therefore, there is a critical public purpose being served by allocating real resources to national defense. The next step is to set the objectives of our defense effort. At one time this included "the ability to fight a prolonged war on two fronts" much like the European and Pacific fronts of World War II. Other objectives have included the ability to strike mostly anywhere in the world within a certain number of hours with a force of a pre-determined size, to maintain air superiority and to be able to deliver nuclear weapons against the Soviet Union and other potentially hostile nations which can direct nuclear weapons at the U.S. and, more recently, to have the capability of using drones to assassinate hostile individuals remotely anywhere in the world.

These are all military objectives. Some are general, some very specific. In the United States, they are ultimately political choices. For me this means the President, as Commander in Chief, submitting these types of high-level military objectives to Congress for approval, and then working to achieve those objectives by proposing more specific military options to accomplish our national goals. The President proposes objectives and what is needed to accomplish those objectives, and the Congress reviews, debates, and modifies the objectives and proposals to meet those objectives, and appropriates the resources it decides necessary to meet what it decides best serves the nation's military objectives.

Most of the world's democracies (and particularly those with a U.S. military presence) have, however, come to rely on the assumption that the U.S. would ultimately defend them. Often, though not always, this is through formal alliances. This ultimate reliance on the U.S. military has resulted in these nations not allocating what would otherwise be substantial portions of their real wealth to their national defense. One option for addressing this issue would be to meet with the world's democracies and establish what a "fair contribution" to the U.S. defense effort would be for these nations, and then go so far as to publish a "non defense" pledge for those who refuse to contribute their fair share of real goods and services to the common defense.

The 'right sized' defense has everything to do with actual defense needs, and nothing to do with the total expenditures of dollars necessary to meet the nation's defense needs. Nor need there any mention of "how are we going to pay for it" as taxes function to regulate aggregate demand and not to raise revenue per se. The way we, the current generation, always "pay for I'" is by the real resources - goods and services - that are allocated to the military that could have remained in the private sector for private consumption. That real cost includes all the people serving in the military who could have been working and producing goods and services in the private sector for private consumption. That includes everything from auto workers to tennis instructors, lawyers, doctors, and stock brokers.

The "right size" and "right type" of defense can change dramatically over relatively short periods of time. China's capability of shooting down satellites and Iranian medium range nuclear missiles that could threaten our shipping are but two examples of how the advance of military technology can very quickly make prior technologies instantly obsolete. Both objectives and options must be under continuous review, and there can be no let up in advancing new technologies to do all we can to stay on the leading edge of military effectiveness.

About 10 years ago I was discussing the military with a member of the Pentagon. He said that we needed to increase the size of the military. I said that if we wanted to do that we should have done it ten years ago (1990) when we were in a recession with high unemployment and excess capacity in general. Back then, with all that excess capacity, a build up of the military would not have been taking as many productive resources away from the private sector as it would have done during a period of full employment. He responded, "Yes, but back then we couldn't afford it, the nation was running a budget deficit; while today with a budget surplus, we can afford it'. This is completely backwards! The government never has nor doesn't have any dollars. The right amount of spending has nothing to do with whether the budget is in surplus or deficit. They use the monetary system which provides no information for all their information.

## Inflation!

OK, so the risk of running a deficit that is too large is not insolvency - the government can't go broke - but excess aggregate demand (spending power) that can be inflationary. While this is something I've never seen in the U.S. in my 60-year lifetime, it is theoretically possible. But then again, this can only happen if the government doesn't limit its spending by the prices it is willing to pay, and, instead, is willing to pay ever higher prices even as it's spending drives up those prices, as would probably the case.

And now here is a good place to review what I first wrote back in 1992 for *Soft Currency Economics* which came out in 1993:

### Inflation vs. Price Increases

Bottom line, the currency itself is a public monopoly, which means the price level is necessarily a function of prices paid by the government when it spends, and/or collateral demanded when it lends. The last part means that if the Fed simply lent without limit and without demanding collateral we would all borrow like crazy and drive prices to the moon. Hence, bank assets need to be regulated because otherwise, with FDIC-insured deposits, bankers could and probably would borrow like crazy to pay themselves unlimited salaries at taxpayer expense. And that's pretty much what happened in the S & L crisis of the 1980's, which also helped drive the Reagan boom until it was discovered. Much like the sub prime boom drove the Bush expansion until it was discovered. So it now goes without saying that bank assets and capital ratios need to be regulated.

But let's return to the first part of the statement - "the price level is a function of prices paid by govt. when it spends." What does this mean? It means that since the economy needs the government spending to get the dollars it needs to pay taxes, the government can, as a point of logic decide what it wants to pay for things, and the economy has no choice but to sell to the government at the prices set by government in order to get the dollars it needs to pay taxes, and save however many dollar financial assets it wants to. Let me give you an extreme example of how this works: Suppose the government said it wasn't going to pay a penny more for anything this year than it paid last year, and was going to leave taxes as they are in any case. And then suppose this year all prices went up by more than that. In that case, with its policy of not paying a penny more for anything, government would decide that spending would go from last year's $3.5 trillion to 0. That would leave the private sector trillions of dollars short of the funds it needs to pay the taxes. To get the funds needed to pay its taxes, prices would start falling in the economy as people offered their unsold goods and services at lower and lower prices until they got back to last year's prices and the government then bought them. While that's a completely impractical way to keep prices going up, in a market economy, the government would only have to do that with one price, and let market forces adjust all other prices to reflect relative values. Historically, this type of arrangement has been applied in what are called "buffer stock" policies, and were mainly done with agricultural products, whereby the government might set a prices for wheat at which it will buy or sell. The gold standard is also an example of a buffer stock policy.

Today's governments unofficially use unemployment as their buffer stock policy. The theory is that the price level in general is a function of the level of unemployment, and the way to control inflation is through the employment rate. The tradeoff becomes higher unemployment vs.

114

higher inflation. To say this policy is problematic is a gross understatement, but no one seems to have any alternative that's worthy of debate.

All the problematic inflation I've seen has been caused by rising energy prices, which begins as a relative value story but soon gets passed through to most everything and turns into an inflation story. The "pass through" mechanism, the way I see it, comes from government paying higher prices for what it buys, including indexing government wages to the CPI (Consumer Price Index), which is how we as a nation have chosen to define inflation. And every time the government pays more for the same thing, it is redefining its currency downward.

It is like the parents with the kids who need to do chores to earn the coupons they need to pay the monthly tax to their parents. What is the value of those coupons? If the parents pay one coupon for an hour's worth of work (and all the work is about equally difficult and equally "unpleasant"), then one coupon will be worth an hour's worth of child labor. And if the children were to exchange coupons with each other, that's how they would value them. Now suppose that the parents paid two coupons for an hour's worth of work. In that case, each coupon is only worth a half hour's worth of work. By paying twice as many coupons for the same amount of work, the parents caused the value of the coupons to drop in half.

But what we have is a government that doesn't understand its own monetary operations, so, in America, the seven deadly innocent frauds rule. Our leaders think they need to tax to get the dollars to spend, and what they don't tax they have to borrow from the likes of China and stick our children with the tab. And they think they have to pay market prices. So from there the policy becomes one of not letting the economy get too good, not letting unemployment get too low, or else we risk a sudden hyperinflation like the

Weimar Republic in Germany 100 years or so ago. Sad but true. So today, we sit with unemployment pushing 20% if you count people who can't find full-time work, maybe 1/3 of our productive capacity going idle, and with a bit of very modest GDP growth - barely enough to keep unemployment from going up. And no one in Washington thinks it's unreasonable for the Fed to be on guard over inflation and ready to hike rates to keep things from overheating (not that rate hikes do that, but that's another story).

And what is the mainstream theory about inflation? It's called "expectations theory." For all but a few of us, inflation is caused entirely by rising inflation expectations. It works this way: when people think there is going to be inflation, they demand pay increases and rush out to buy things before the price goes up. And that's what causes inflation. What's called a "falling output gap," which means falling unemployment for all practical purposes, is what causes inflation expectations to rise. And foreign monopolists hiking oil prices can make inflation expectations rise, as can people getting scared over budget deficits, or getting scared by the Fed getting scared. So the job of the Fed regarding inflation control becomes managing inflation expectations. That's why with every Fed speech there's a section about how they are working hard to control inflation, and how important that is. They also believe that the direction of the economy is dependent on expectations, so they will always forecast "modest growth" or better, which they believe helps to cause that outcome. And they will never publicly forecast a collapse, because they believe that that could cause a collapse all by itself.

So for me, our biggest inflation risk now, as in the 1970's, is energy prices (particularly gasoline). Inflation will come through the cost side, from a price-setting group of producers, and not from market forces or excess demand. Strictly speaking, it's a relative value story and not an inflation story, at least initially, which then becomes an inflation story as the higher imported costs work their way through our price structure with government doing more than its share of paying those higher prices and thereby redefining its currency downward in the process.